BALANDA

BALANDA

My Year in Arnhem Land

MARY ELLEN JORDAN

ALLEN&UNWIN

ARTS VICTORIA

First published in 2005

Allen & Unwin
83 Alexander Street
Crows Nest NSW 2065
Australia
Phone: (61 2) 8425 0100
Fax: (61 2) 9906 2218
Email: info@allenandunwin.com
Web: www.allenandunwin.com

National Library of Australia
Cataloguing-in-Publication entry:

Jordan, Mary Ellen.
   Balanda, my year in Arnhem Land.

   ISBN 978 1 74114 280 8

   1. Jordan, Mary Ellen – Journeys – Northern Territory –
   Arnhem Land. 2. Arts, Aboriginal Australian – Northern
   Territory – Maningrida. 3. Aboriginal Australians -
   Northern Territory – Arnhem Land – Social conditions. 4.
   Arnhem Land (N.T.) – Biography. I. Title.

994.29507092

Set in 12/16 pt Adobe Jenson Pro by Bookhouse, Sydney
Printed in Australia by McPherson's Printing Group

10 9 8 7 6 5 4 3

Balanda: the word used by Aboriginal people in the north of the Northern Territory to refer to non-Aboriginal people.

It is one of several words of Indonesian found in the Aboriginal languages of the Top End.

For a couple of hundred years before Captain Cook landed, Macassans would sail down from Indonesia to Arnhem Land on the annual monsoon winds to harvest *trepang*, a kind of sea slug, establishing trade and cultural exchange with the locals; *Balanda* comes from the Macassan word 'Hollander', for their Dutch colonisers.

Author's note

THIS BOOK IS ABOUT THE TIME I SPENT LIVING AND WORKING in Maningrida, in Arnhem Land. It is a subjective, personal account—the story of what it was like for me to live in that particular community, at that time. I have selected what to write about on the basis of how interesting it was for me, or how it made me think and changed my opinions, or how it fitted in to the rest of the story; this doesn't necessarily make for an objective, even-handed account.

To protect the privacy of the many people I lived alongside, and particularly those who gave me friendship, company and invaluable experiences while I was there, I have not only changed the names of characters, but blended them, stripped them back, changed them—I have endeavoured to create typical characters, rather than depicting actual people. The events I describe, however, actually occurred.

This is my story. The stories of other people who were there at the same time, whether Aboriginal or Balanda (European), would be different. And none of them would be wrong.

Since I lived in Maningrida, there has been a substantial change in the administration of the funding of Aboriginal communities. In 2004 the Australian Government disbanded ATSIC, the Aboriginal and Torres Strait Islander Commission. ATSIC was run by elected representatives of Aboriginal people from all over Australia, and managed the funding for Aboriginal programs except those for health, which were managed by the federal department responsible for health. These programs have now been incorporated into the relevant 'mainstream' government departments.

One

JUST BEYOND THE TOWN, PAST THE FIRE TOWER ON THE WIDE DIRT road we call the highway, the Aboriginal world begins. Here in the town there are tame streets recently asphalted into permanence—the roadworkers left last week. Here in the town the grids laid out for houses force people to walk in straight lines, the same straight lines over and over again. We all traverse these streets: we all dodge the pothole on the road to the airport, leap or drive over the dip near the turn-off to the petrol shop and the workshops and the tucker run. Town has its distinct pockets and we move between them regulated by the geometry of Balanda planning. Every road is trees felled, every building is something strange that we brought with us and pressed onto the land. In the farthest corner of the town, the place we call bottom camp, the Dkurridji live. This was their land. We say that it still is, calling them the 'TOs', Balanda shorthand for 'traditional owners'. Everyone who lives in the town,

1

the Aboriginal people from the different parts of Arnhem Land and the outsiders—us, from different parts of the globe—pays a tithe to the Dkurridji in return for their suffering our presence.

This place used to be called Mang djang karirra: the place where the Dreaming changed shape. Said fast, with the cling of familiarity running its syllables together, it turned into Manaying-karírra. And when the Balandas arrived, pale people from different places with tongues that couldn't make the right sounds, this word became Maningrida. It changes again when I say it to people in Melbourne: 'Maningrida', I say, and 'Maningrita', they reply.

I can't work out whether this land still belongs to the Dkurridji—they have people on most committees; they get $6 out of each town resident's pay each fortnight; their houses are on the waterfront, the only beautiful part of town; and the names for the museum and the school newspaper come from their language. Or does it belong to the Balandas, with its roads, cars, buildings of concrete and corrugated iron, shops and garbage bins and barge landing? Have we kept the old names for new things—and changed the taste of the words forever? This used to be the place where the Dreaming changed shape. Now it is the place where the Dreaming mutates, might wither and die, might implode or explode or combust. The continuity and perpetuity of ever-changing shapes might have been distorted into a writhing motion. Is this the place where the Dreaming became a nightmare?

In some ways, everything here is Aboriginal. It is unlike anywhere else I've ever been. Things Balandas take for granted are taken by a Dkurridji and recast, so they wear underpants rolled onto their heads like scarves, and dozens of people live in houses designed for no more than six. To them, clothes are merely practical, while we try to express our identity through labels and colours and styles. They take our language and remove everything extraneous, dropping into it a kind of poetry. One man has a car accident in his resplendent new four-wheel drive and describes it as *that tree bin punchim that car*. My own language and culture are transformed, reinterpreted—it's a place where everything is changing shape.

There is no polishing and pruning and coveting and maintaining of things here—they are seen as transitory, separate from the people who use them. Aboriginal people live around their houses as much as in them, setting up kitchens in the dust. The campfires are lit in the late afternoon all over town, and the smell of burning mangrove wood fills the air like incense, musty. People bring televisions outside and watch them: to someone driving past, they look like squares of purple fluorescence in the night.

Meetings are held under the mango trees. People turn up and sit with their kin, each group oriented to sit closest to their country. Everyone speaks in their own language, assuming the others will understand.

Here, we all know each other by our cars, and as Balandas drive through the town Aboriginal people will sometimes signal to us with their hands, not a wave but a request to stop to talk. 'You Balandas,' we're told by bemused locals, 'always waving!'

There is a sign language used in tandem with words here. There are different languages like rivers through the place, and I understand just a few words of them. A tiny minority of us use English first and foremost; the others speak their own version of English, and use it only when they need to. Balandas grow accustomed to being surrounded by conversations full of words we can't understand.

We pick up phrases from Aboriginal English. I keep asking questions, and often when I'm trying to understand something new I will compare it to something else. 'So it's the same as this?' I'll ask. 'Yeah, same . . .' I'm told, and I think maybe I've finally got it; and then, after a pause, '. . . but different'. Eventually I learn that this is a phrase used deliberately, not a mistake made by people who don't speak English all that well. Same; but different.

I think of this as I watch the opening ceremony for the first remote area Centrelink—the government's welfare shop front— in the Territory. Workmen have been renovating one end of the old council offices for weeks. I can see the aqua and orange colour scheme from my lounge room: it is the same as Centrelinks everywhere—the one around the corner from where I used to live in Fitzroy, inner Melbourne, and the one in Darwin. Inside, there are computers and bench tops and racks of crisp pamphlets, printed in English, yet to wilt and grow mould in the humidity. In the middle of this ceremony are the town's brand new

Centrelink Balanda, who has been given a small demountable crate of a house to live in, and the three Aboriginal trainee staff. They're wearing matching poly-cotton short-sleeved polo shirts.

There will be speeches, which we will ignore or quickly forget. A couple of hundred people are here to see the dancing. This Centrelink is on land owned by the Dkurridji clan and they are going to dance its opening for us. The dance will be taken from the ancient diplomacy ceremonies practised in this region for centuries. We will see a truncated chunk of performance, snatched like a sound bite out of an original ceremony that would have lasted for weeks and weeks.

The dancing is going to begin at 12, and after that, a sausage sizzle, which is being set up fifty metres away. Regulation public event catering in Maningrida: barbecued sausages in bread, pieces of fruit and Popper fruit juice. I'm always hungry at this time of day and I'm distracted by the promise of food.

A bunch of camp dogs wanders among the crowd, making me feel uneasy. Usually starved, sick and craven, some of the town's dogs have lately been running in packs, charged with aggression and a drug called Ivomec that makes them healthy. I've been kept awake at night by their howling. But these dogs are the passive type. They look awful, many of them with no fur left and wounds on their skin, and they slink off as soon as you snarl at them. We call the worst of them 'leatherjackets' and we keep our distance.

The speeches begin against the smell of sausages; the staff are introduced, standing shyly in the centre of the space in the crowd. And then the dancing begins. I've seen this kind of thing before: men in nagas (loincloths) with white ochre smeared on their skin and hair, dancing a kind of symbol of a particular animal. Sometimes it's easy to pick the species, sometimes I need to be told. Often I forget about meaning and watch their feet thwacking the ground amidst small clouds of dust. Off to one side, other men sing, play the didjeridu or the clapsticks. Their music is utterly unlike ours: it sounds as unalike as their languages sound to English.

I am expecting to see the usual stuff, but when the dancing finally begins—well past twelve o'clock—there seems to be something else going on. Men are dancing with spears held high . . . it's clear that this is a story. Someone is a turtle, and he's good, he's really good, and the crowd is leaning forward and calling out. We are watching a battle. It must be out to sea, with the hunters and the turtle. The Balandas can see that the Aboriginal people who know the story are looking forward to the good bit: they cry out, and then we all do. What's happening? Is he a fish? A person? Look at that! I don't understand everything but I can feel the drama rush up my spine, and I am leaning forward and craning my neck and gasping like everyone else. Four women run forward and surround the turtle, emptying their dilly bags. Something about a sacred dilly bag? Something about the Dreaming, of course, but what? The star of the show is cheered, it's all over too soon. As always, I'm amazed by the informality that surrounds ceremony. People stand around beforehand, and the action builds slowly. And afterwards, the performers melt into the crowd, striking figures in ochre and nagas with spears in their hands, but standing alongside everyone else. And like everyone else, they're heading for the sausages, which are probably not ready yet.

We're all mingling, deciding whether to hold out for the barbecue or head home for lunch, chatting and admiring what we have just seen. There are kids everywhere; dogs everywhere; all the town's languages, including both kinds of English, flying through the air. The Balanda who works for the council is gladhanding the visitors.

The Centrelink is now open and there are people walking through it. I glance in the window: the only thing that sets it apart from other Centrelinks is how strange it looks in these surroundings, a bright shiny thing attached to a dilapidated building. The credit union next door is always chaotic, a huge room full of dogs and people waiting to be served by scant staff. It is also an agent for the post office, so I've been there a few times. Whenever I stand back behind the customers crowding around the counter I wonder whether this is an Aboriginal way of managing a queue, or whether it's as chaotic as it looks, with no sense of who was here first or who will be served next. I don't know how to do it—am I supposed to stand back, or to push to the front? Usually I give up and walk away, my Balanda imperative to work efficiently clicking away in time with the passing minutes.

The ground around Centrelink is dusty and unplanted. There are half a dozen garbage bins here that get turned over every weekend by bored kids. The muddy-coloured art centre looms behind the aqua blob of bureaucracy. It looks comical, perfect for a city street, but transplanted out here where things are different. People are saying what a great idea this Centrelink is. I have been here a year now, long enough to have my doubts. As with all the great ideas that are talked about here, the first step is a new Balanda to run things, and the second step is a new building for them to live in.

∽ ∾

When I got here, I vaguely expected the community to be a mishmash of black and white—but in fact there is a sharp social divide. I had thought that the white people, a tenth or less of the community, would have both black and white friends, but we socialise among ourselves, while the Aboriginal communities keep to themselves. There is a lot of interaction, but most of it takes place around work—teaching, project managing, building or buying and selling.

When I decided to leave Melbourne for Maningrida, I thought that Balandas like me would be working alongside Aboriginal people, assisting them to run their community org-anisations. I came here to do this, with good intentions and the expectation of being of some use. I thought that self-determination meant that Aboriginal people would be in charge, and that with funding and support from white Australia, things would get better for communities like this.

But nothing here is that simple. I'm still learning what it means to be a Balanda, and slowly putting together my own patchwork of understandings and confusions about this one part of Aboriginal Australia.

As a Balanda, I collect the glimpses I get of the Aboriginal communities across the cultural divide. We smile across our differences, and work across them, and talk and laugh and compromise across them. In some ways, we're all the same. Same—but different.

Two

I WAS LEAVING FAMILIARITY BEHIND. THE PLANE SEATED TWENTY people in the smallest possible space, as though someone had taken the seats and shrunk a shell around them. It was taking me to Maningrida, a place I had no image of. I hadn't seen any photos or heard any descriptions. If I tried to picture it, all I came up with was white noise. When the pilot announced our descent into Maningrida, it felt like reaching the horizon. I'd been in Darwin for the few days since leaving Melbourne, adjusting to the heat and buying supplies. Now after an hour's journey, the plane dipped and tilted over a wide bright blue rivermouth and then in towards the town, perched on the eastern bank. I was surprised by the sparkling beauty of water and sky. Some of my anxiety lifted—surely beauty like this could sustain me. Still, I was all nerves and newness and timidity. I didn't know exactly what I would be doing in this town and I didn't know whether I would be any good at it. Now there was no more time to worry.

We'd landed, the little tin-shed airport was getting closer and my friend Alice had just driven up and got out of her four-wheel drive. I took a deep breath. *I'm here.*

Walking towards me was a tall, slim woman, with shoulder-length dark brown hair that fanned out in curls around her face when it wasn't tied back out of the way. She was dressed in knee-length shorts, a t-shirt and boots. We went to university together and hadn't seen each other for a few years. She and her partner Mal, who ran the Jobs, Education and Training Centre (JET), had been here for about a year, and had worked in another community in the Northern Territory before that. She ran the art centre where I was about to start work, and she was the only person I knew in Maningrida.

After we'd said hello, I exclaimed, 'This is so far away.'

Alice laughed and replied, 'No, other places are far from here. Here is just here.'

We climbed into her old vehicle and she took me on a tour of the town, driving along the main dirt road. It was all so different. I had to hold onto my nerves and try to keep my anxieties contained. I pushed them down so that my words could come out clearly, without anxiety's pitch stretching them up into the sound of what I really felt.

The houses were surrounded by naked ground rather than grass or gardens. Everything seemed to be the same dusty brownish orange colour. A rusty old tower loomed up in the part of town Alice called the 'industrial precinct'—a relic from another era, when there was an attempt to create a forestry industry. Makeshift sheds surrounded by cyclone fencing, this part of town was now used for workshops for the house builders, plumbers, road builders and mechanics who worked for the community. The houses, which were completely unadorned, were made of concrete blocks or tin, the painted ones faded to dull shades of yellow, green or blue. They were lined up close together without fences, looking stark and crowded at the same time. The architecture reminded me of the tin portable rooms we used as classrooms at high school. Some of the houses we passed were 'demountables', but even the permanent dwellings had the temporary, utilitarian, tin-shed appearance of the portables. There was rubbish all over the ground, and only a few trees, spindly eucalypts that didn't improve things much. Some places had decrepit furniture propped up outside—the skeleton of an old table, or a chair without its stuffing. It was like a parody of suburbia.

Around the corner it got worse: three shed-like houses, with gaping holes for windows and burnt-out doorframes, and graffiti on the walls. Alice explained that these were old structures that had been replaced, although overcrowding meant that people still used them sometimes. These houses were in a better setting, with trees and grass and open space around them. A group of about two dozen adults sat in a circle, surrounded by children. I asked Alice what they were doing. 'Playing cards' she said. Gambling on card games, I found out later, was one of the major leisure activities in the town.

Down another dirt road Alice pointed out the Maningrida Progress Association, a four-room hotel for visiting officials, bureaucrats and researchers, a takeaway called Hasty Tasty and a shop. All these businesses were run by the Maningrida Progress Association, which returned all profits to the community. The buildings that housed them were all low-slung, grey or brown, and without any of the cultural trappings I was used to. The squat building with barred windows was not something I would have recognised as a shop. Across the road was an open space, where the Dry Season had sapped the green out of the grass, leaving a dusty brown square behind.

We passed the school, another collection of shabby buildings surrounded by dust, and reached the art centre, another low, tin-roofed, brown brick and concrete building. Alice told me that it shared its premises with Bawinanga Aboriginal Corporation, its parent body. Bawinanga was a resource agency that supported Aboriginal people to live on their own land in the thirty outstations that had been established for different clans on their country surrounding Maningrida.

Alice stopped the car and we got out. This was the place I'd be working in for the next year. Inside was old grey lino, worn-out laminex bench tops and a shabby collection of office furniture. The cheap grey desks looked about twenty years old, and the vinyl seats on the chairs were split. The floor was maroon-painted concrete, and the once-white walls were unevenly grey. Despite its unpromising appearance, it was full of the smell of pandanus, reeds and wood. Countless bark paintings leant against the walls in stacks, and shelves full of baskets filled one corner of a warehouse. The plants had been treated, dried out and dyed, transformed into works of art, but still they brought the smells and colours of the bush into the art centre, compensating for the decor.

I met a stream of people whose names fell straight out of my head. Some were white, some were Aboriginal, but nearly all of them seemed to be middle-aged men. By the time Alice took me to my new office and gave me a set of keys, I was too overloaded to take anything in. I was grateful for the suggestion that we go to my flat, so that I could settle in.

My new home was attached to the museum and had two rooms, plus a bathroom. The previous tenant, a man called Simon, expected to come back in about a year, and had left most of his things behind. Alice opened all the windows and turned on the ceiling fans to dispel the stuffy, three-weeks-empty air, and then gave me a tour. In the bedroom was a gun safe. It looked a bit like a locker, made of grey-green metal and about as tall as me. Alice opened the door to reveal a rifle and a hand gun. The sight of them shocked and frightened me, bringing another image to mind: my parents' bedroom when I was four—the doorway, the wardrobe on the left-hand wall, and two rifles in the corner of the wardrobe.

'Why does Simon have a gun safe?' I asked, pushing the memory away.

'It's a new law in the Territory,' Alice replied, locking the safe.

'Yes,' I said, 'but why does he have guns?'

'They're for hunting. Most of the blokes up here are into that sort of thing.'

I took the key off my new key ring and asked Alice to keep it at her house.

Alice left me to unpack and I started to explore, moving like a tentative guest. The main room was a kitchen and living area, with louvre windows on both sides. There were no windows in the bedroom, where a dusty fan moved the air around. Off the bedroom was a lobby with doors to the museum, the bathroom and outside. The bathroom looked older than the rest of the flat—years of Wet and Dry seasons had peeled the paint and added mould to the white and green walls. It felt like a public shower block, with a changing cubicle in front of the shower, and the toilet and hand basin each in another cubicle. They were lined up like train carriages, with doorways between them and a corridor running down the side.

In the rest of the flat, the walls were white, but the doors and window frames were all a dark brownish maroon. A big cane blind covered one bank of windows, and the opposite set faced the verandah, which was enclosed by dark grey plastic army-style camouflage netting, thick with dust and the tendrils of an overgrown creeper. The flat was stuffy, dark and plain, but I reminded myself that it was much better than most of what I'd seen in the town.

It felt like someone else's house. A notice board in the loo had postcards and cartoons and tickets to a Bob Dylan concert pinned on it. In the kitchen I peered at images of Pacific islands Simon had left stuck to the fridge, and then opened it to find strange jars of pickles, rosella jam and murky chutney. There was food in the cupboard, and dishes in the draining rack. In the three weeks since Simon had left, the whole place had acquired a coating of dust and spider webs. I wiped down the benches and began to unpack. I put the cups I brought from home on the bench, but not in the cupboard. In the bedroom I covered the gun safe with a blue and white sarong and put a pile of books on top of it, turning it into a simple shelf. It seemed premature to take my clothes out of the backpack. Could it really be that I lived here now?

∽ ∾

Alice came back after a few hours to take me to her house for dinner. She and Mal lived in the part of town where both Balanda and Aboriginal people lived. On the streets were Balanda houses, with fences and gardens kept green during the Dry Season with daily watering, alongside Aboriginal houses with no fences, where people sat around a fire outside and the ground was dusty and dry, and dogs lay in cowed heaps on the verandahs. I met Mal, a thin man who seemed to be a foot taller than Alice, with receding light brown hair cut short against his head. Their house was designed by Troppo, architects who were famous for design suited to the tropical climate. One wall of the main room was fly-wire, open onto empty land running towards the river in the distance. The house was on stilts, and there were gaps between the floorboards so that air could circulate under the house and up through the floor. Every wall had glass or wooden louvres so they could be opened or closed depending on the season. Although it was a fairly plain house, furnished in much the same way as my flat, the design itself was so much better than anything else I'd seen that it stood out as almost beautiful compared with the concrete and tin boxes that lined most of the streets. It felt lofty, light and airy—a sanctuary away from the ugliness of the rest of the town.

Alice and Mal had several friends staying from Melbourne, doing various jobs in the art centre, including taking photos for the book that I was to be working on. Dinner with a big group of Melbournites should have been a familiar experience, but even there I felt out of place. The guests were all having a good time, and they talked about their experiences enthusiastically. The photographers wanted to get out and take photos of the weavers using their baskets, instead of just taking studio shots. People were laughing easily about how many dogs there were in the shop this afternoon, and how expensive the corn chips were. I laughed along with the jokes and listened intently, trying to get some clues from these visitors as to what a life in Maningrida might be like.

Mal drove me home after dinner, his headlamps lighting the otherwise deserted area around the museum. My flat was surrounded by administrative buildings and the school, with no immediate neighbours. As Mal drove away I hurried inside, anxious to close the door on so much unlit empty space. Later, I got into a strange bed made up with the blue sheets I had brought with me, and listened to the night sounds: kids squealing on the basketball courts; a dog barking; an occasional bird call; the quiet hum of the ceiling fan. My brain was stretched out like a fake smile. I was overwhelmed by the detail of being there, and unable to process it. Thoughts of tomorrow and what it might hold crowded my head until finally I fell asleep.

I could see the art centre from my kitchen window, less than a minute's walk away. But I wasn't going to work on my first day; the whole morning was organised around a visit to the shop. It was open from 10 a.m. to 12 p.m. and 2 p.m. to 5 p.m. each weekday, and from 10 a.m. to 12 p.m. every second Saturday. It was five minutes' walk from my flat, halfway to Alice and Mal's house. My steps were tentative—I was aware that I was being tolerated on Aboriginal land. A Balanda needs a permit to even be in Arnhem Land, and I'd been told I would need to ask permission when leaving the town to enter someone's country. I'd never been part of such a small minority before—there were 100–150 Balandas in a community of around 1500.

On the way to the shop, my Melbourne eyes were startled by the sight of so many dark faces, all of them the deepest and richest shades of blackish brown. My skin is the kind that burns easily and never tans; surely to the Aboriginal people I must have looked like a pale imitation of a human. As a brand new Balanda, I felt conspicuous.

When I got there I found a crowd of people with lots of kids and dogs milling around the entrance. My vague expectation of an informal general store floated away as I entered the stark concrete shell, with metal security mesh surrounding the areas where cigarettes and other expensive items were sold. The rest of the goods were arranged on shelves, often in their packing boxes. There was a whole aisle of chips and soft drinks, and a section selling white sugar in 5 kilo tins. There were also huge tins of milk powder and other groceries that keep: canned things and dried things. Along the back wall were the freezers and fridges, where there were basic dairy products, a small selection of fruit and vegetables, and frozen meat and various frozen foods. Everything seemed incredibly expensive, no doubt to cover the cost of getting it all in on the barge. In Darwin, most groceries were around 50 cents more than in Melbourne; in Maningrida, they cost much more, sometimes one and a half times as much as I was used to.

For the rest of the morning I cleaned out the kitchen. I took everything out of the cupboards and wiped them down, but they still smelt of mould left behind by previous Wet Seasons. I chose the best of Simon's kitchenware and put it with the things I'd brought from home in the least smelly cupboard. I stuck photos of friends and family on the fridge; I thought about rearranging the furniture. I grappled with dust, which seemed to be a big part of Maningrida life. As I was to discover, anything left alone for long enough—windows, cars, outdoor furniture—would get a layer of dust like thick paint. Sponges came away from bench tops with a dark brownish-red smear across them. Any cleaning task involved dust-filled sneezes. After only a morning, my sandals had absorbed a permanent sheen of it, dulling their soft blue colour into a nondescript grey. Alice had told me to take my shoes off when I went inside, to avoid bringing too much of the dust in, partly because it incubated various diseases. I remembered that in Melbourne a woman had told me to be careful—she had got chlamydia in her eye while living in an Aboriginal community, the infection transported in the dust.

Alice had introduced me to everyone by saying that I was there for a few months to work on a book about weaving in central Arnhem Land. She and I had agreed previously that if I liked it, I would stay and take on the job of cultural researcher, which hadn't been filled since Simon left. As well as buying and selling art, the art centre's charter included cultural maintenance and support, which was why there was a cultural office. This office documented the art work, ran the museum and kept a shelf full of books relevant to the local cultures, dictionary databases, an archive of photographs and some recordings of music. It was a safe-keeping place for records of culture.

For my first few days, I spent most of my time in the culture office trying to get my head around the file relating to the book project. The more I delved, the more complicated the book project seemed to be. It had stalled with only a very early draft. I decided that if I could get this done then I would have achieved something worthwhile with my time in the community. I talked to Alice a lot, amazed by how confident and comfortable she was in a world that seemed utterly foreign to me. I was relying on her experience and judgement as I felt my way.

∽ ∾

On my third day, Alice told me about a language project that had just been funded to produce learners' guides and dictionaries for six of the local languages. Bawinanga had applied for funding under the Language Access Initiative, which was money the government had allocated for cultural maintenance in response to *Bringing Them Home*, the Stolen Generations report. The money was administered by ATSIC, the Aboriginal and Torres Strait Islander Commission.

I asked how much they had applied for.

'A million dollars,' she replied.

I was incredulous.

Then she added, 'We've got $190,000 over two years.'

When she showed me the grant application, the million-dollar budget made sense. In this document Alice had set out the grand vision for the project: indigenous speakers and language workers working with a linguist on each of six languages, full time, for two years. It easily added up to a million dollars.

'We need to scale this down so it can be run from the culture office on a fifth of the budget,' Alice said. She thought it was still feasible to produce some kind of dictionary and learners' guide for each language. Most of the languages had been studied by linguists already—this project would be a chance to take their notes, records and databases and turn them into products that the communities could use. There were already dictionaries for the three biggest languages—Burarra, Kuninjku and Ndjébbana—so this funding was for the smaller languages: Nakara, Rembarrnga, Djinang, Dalabon, Gurrgoni and Kunbarlang.

I liked the way Alice had designed the project. She described it as 'community-oriented'—it was about making resources that Aboriginal people would find useful, rather than about documenting the languages for documentation's own sake. The aim was to make bilingual dictionaries with explanations in plain English, and learners' guides written in a simple and accessible way.

Training Aboriginal people was also an important part of this project. Alice wanted linguists to pass on techniques for recording and documenting languages to the speakers. Helping the community to preserve their own languages was a particularly exciting part of the plan.

I asked who would be the coordinator, and Alice looked at me. This was an exciting prospect—I had a degree in linguistics and I had come to Maningrida thinking that I might end up working on one of these languages, if there was a group of speakers who wanted to work with a linguist—but at the same time it was terrifying. It felt huge, and I felt I was utterly inexperienced and had no idea where to begin. But this was obviously going to be the main focus in the culture office for the next couple of years. If I stayed more than a few months, I would definitely be coordinating this project.

Later, I was immersed in trying to understand the complexities of the weaving book when one of the middle-aged men I had met on my first day came in.

'Hi Archie,' Alice said, reminding me that he was Bawinanga's project coordinator. This seemed to include building and maintaining outstations and running the Community Development and Employment Project (CDEP), which had been described to me as being a bit like a 'work-for-the-dole' scheme, but exclusively for Aboriginal communities. People on the scheme signed up to work twenty hours per week, and they got the same amount as the dole. All this was funded by ATSIC. Archie was tall and had a long grey beard and a large pot belly and was dressed in a polo shirt and shorts—standard Balanda male attire.

'Just reminding you that you'll need to do a provisional budget for the language project,' he said.

'Right. When does it need to be in?' Alice asked.

'End of the month,' he answered. Then he grinned and added, 'It's just a formality.'

When Archie left, Alice explained that ATSIC had offered us the funding, but to secure it we needed to send them a budget outlining how it would be spent.

'Why did he say it was just a formality?' I asked. Alice told me that Bawinanga had had millions of dollars in funding from ATSIC over the years, and had always spent it properly, accounted for it and fulfilled the requirements of the grants.

This gave Bawinanga a better record than most Aboriginal organisations. Bawinanga knew how to run a project and spend funding, so ATSIC liked giving it money. In this case, 'Bawinanga' meant Alice and me. We set to work with the grant application, a calculator and notepads. Dividing, multiplying and adding hypothetical work hours for linguists, trainees and speakers, we reached $95,000 very quickly. It no longer looked like a huge amount of money.

When Archie saw the budget, he told me to simplify it. It ended up being a neat table with seven items, described in a couple of words, adding up to the right amount. Somehow I needed to take us from this single sheet of paper to a set of dictionaries and learners' guides for six languages, whose speakers

I had not even met. As soon as the weaving book was running smoothly, it would be time to start thinking about languages.

∽ ∾

In among the budgeting, I met the art centre's most famous artist. Jimmy was about to go to Sydney for a solo show. His paintings had been sent there already, but Alice still needed to write a documentation to go with one of them. She brought out a blurry digital photograph of the painting and asked Jimmy to tell her its story. I was expected to learn to write documentations because this was an important part of the cultural researcher's job, and this was my introduction to the process.

Jimmy spoke Aboriginal English with a very heavy accent, and used his words sparingly. He spoke reluctantly, releasing words in short bursts like coveted secrets. He had a thin face, surrounded by unruly wooly hair. He was wearing a baggy faded shirt and shorts, without shoes. I could hardly understand a thing he said.

One of my reasons for going to Maningrida was an awareness of how little I knew about Aboriginal cultures, and a desire to learn more. Like many white Australians, I had heard about the complex spirituality and religion of these cultures, particularly about the Dreaming and the deep relationship to land. At university, I had learnt about phenomenally complex languages and kinship systems. These snippets of knowledge made me aware of how little I knew about Jimmy's culture, and how easy it would be for me to say the wrong thing, ask a rude question or be offensive in some other way. Just as I couldn't speak his language—in fact, I'd only just learnt to spell it (Kuninjku)—I was entirely ignorant of his culture. I was intimidated into silence.

Alice, however, carried on a conversation seemingly effortlessly—she knew some of Jimmy's language. She also knew about this particular painting, asking questions like, 'And these circles here, are they that bangkarl plant?' Jimmy nodded his head vigorously and said 'Yo, yo' (yes, yes). Alice's questions were all leading questions, asking for confirmation of what she already knew. How would I ever be able to do this?

They finished with a simple exchange: 'Ma. Bobo.' These words were easy to learn, because Balandas picked up on them and used them with each other. 'Ma' meant 'OK' or 'that's enough', and I'd learnt 'bobo' for goodbye by hearing it from Alice and Mal and other Balandas.

෩ ෩

My fourth morning was barge morning. Mal called me at 8 a.m., saying I should come with him to pick up his groceries so I could learn how it was done. He told me that it was the big Balanda social event of the week. For a new girl, this was an enticing prospect.

The barge came in every Thursday at the landing, about 200 metres from my house, arriving on the tide—so it could unload any time between about 6 and 10 a.m. Most of the Balandas in town ordered their groceries from Coles in Darwin, who put them on the barge. I thought that was why it was such a big event—everyone would be there to collect their shopping.

We drove up and parked among the dozen other four-wheel drive trucks. Then we climbed up to the captain's office to collect Mal's 'manifest'. This turned out to be a docket telling you what was on the barge for you, and which containers it was in. I hadn't expected the barge to be so big—it seemed more like a ship. The back came down onto the landing like a drawbridge so that the forklifts could drive the containers ashore for unloading. We had to climb three or four metal ladders to reach the office—I realised I should never wear a skirt for this again. I reminded myself not to look down as we walked along a narrow gangway at the side of the barge, high above the water on one side and forklifts scurrying between the containers on the other.

Back on the ground, Mal introduced me to a few locals— and my impression that every white person in town was a middle-aged man was only reinforced. There were almost no women there.

Finally, I saw why. The deliveries from Coles were only a tiny proportion of what the barge was disgorging. There were also pallets loaded with food for the shop, the takeaway outlet and the school tuckshop. There were all kinds of building materials, from pipes to sacks of concrete to toilets, and there were cars and car parts. And there were huge quantities of all of it. It seemed that most of the Balandas in Maningrida, especially in the Dry Season, were blokes—builders, road workers, mechanics, electricians, plumbers. They collected their groceries as well as their industrial supplies: barge business was men's work.

I was beginning to see that, as a single white woman living alone, I was an oddity. As I would find out, most people were here in couples or families, and the single nurses and teachers either shared houses or lived in adjacent flats. The school's caretaker—a man—picked up the deliveries for all school staff, because they couldn't leave their classrooms for this, and the clinic also sent a couple of people down for all the staff. One of them was a nurse called Sam. She was the only other woman at the barge landing. We introduced ourselves but didn't find much to say to each other. But she said she wanted to come to the art centre to look at our books on the town and its history.

I went home for a quick breakfast before work. Realising that the barge was Maningrida's big social scene, I felt more disheartened than ever—how could I belong in a place like this? I had expected that an Aboriginal community would be full of well-meaning young people who, like me, had been brought here by their social conscience. Instead, it seemed to be a town for the blokiest of blokes—all older than me, bushy, macho and confident in their work and mateship and special blokey ways of communicating.

I felt less disheartened as the day went on. The photographers, Rob and Jess, and Alice and I had planned to take some photos of baskets and fish traps being modelled by the women who made them. An old lady called Nellie had agreed to pose with one of her dilly bags, a long basket with a domed bottom and a string strap. We drove off to Top Camp to find her. Top Camp, Bottom Camp and Side Camp were the Aboriginal parts of town. Nellie's place was close to the airport, and must have been one of the houses I saw when I first arrived. We pulled up outside and called to her—there was no knocking on doors in Maningrida. There was no answer.

Alice thought that Nellie might have been involved in a young men's ceremony that was in progress at the house next door to her so we went and tried there. A roadblock stopped us from driving up to the house—it was against the law to drive through a ceremony ground. A woman called Katie emerged and said that Nellie was in Side Camp, at Johnny's house.

'Which house is that?' we asked.

'That blue downstairs house,' she said. Then she invited us to come back that night and watch the dancing for the ceremony.

We drove off the main road onto one of the dirt tracks that criss-crossed Side Camp and soon found a single-storey house with faded blue paint. Side Camp had the same suburban parody feel as Top Camp, but some of the houses were in better condition and there were more trees and grass around them. And there were more people around—groups of small children playing under a tree, or adults sitting outside alone or in small groups. A group of camp dogs ran up to the car, barking ferociously.

Once again we called out from the road, and once again we were told that Nellie wasn't there. She had left for Top Camp a while ago. We drove back to Top Camp to try one last time. Just as we were ready to give up, we saw Nellie walking down the road towards us. She was in her late fifties, old by Maningrida standards, with a head full of loose, grey-white corkscrew curls. She had a serious face, with a huge, protruding bottom lip that gave her a petulant expression. The afternoon's light was almost gone, and she was too busy with the ceremony for photographs, so there was only time for two or three shots. I'd been told that things worked differently here, but still my city mindset was appalled at how inefficient this process had been. It was hard to accept that making an appointment with somebody, and expecting them to keep it, was not necessarily going to mean that the meeting took place.

By the time we got back to the art centre, the smell of burning mangrove wood was in the air. Each night at 5 or 6 o'clock the campfires were lit. Local people regarded this time of year as cold, so the fires were for warmth as well as for cooking. The pungent, sweet spicy smell of this particular wood reminded me of frankincense, and was becoming the familiar smell of dusk.

∽ ∾

I was in awe watching this, my first Aboriginal ceremony. It was a bit like seeing a foreign film without the sub-titles. Of course, no-one was interpreting or explaining it for us, and I was too new to know what was going on. I was there with Alice and Mal and their friends. Mal sat with the men, some of whom were singing and playing clapsticks and the didjeridu, accompanying the dancing that was the focus.

Alice and I sat on the ground with some young women with small children. Around us the older women were organising food and cooking it at three or four fires. At the fire near us Nellie turned kangaroo tails in the ashes—my first glimpse of 'bush tucker', although Alice told me that these had probably been bought at the local store. Other women stood around the edge of the dancing, doing an accompanying movement with their arms—it looked a bit like rowing. The men in the middle seemed to be dancing a narrative and the kids, too young to take part fully, were joining in and copying and learning how it was done. There was one kid in long grey baggy shorts who danced particularly well and played to the crowd.

The action was sporadic—a small group of men and boys would dance, and then break off, and then dance again, while the music built up and subsided. When the action died down and they took a break I watched the kids, in bright American basketball singlets, run to drink from their bottles of Coke and chatter amongst themselves in a language I couldn't understand. It struck me as the ultimate postmodern scene: an Aboriginal kid with a kangaroo tail in one hand and a bottle of Coke in the other.

It felt exciting to be surrounded by kids who didn't speak English, and it seemed amazing that the culture was so strong still. Having learnt so much about the decline of indigenous languages, especially studying linguistics at university, I didn't expect to see Burarra being passed on with no thought for English at all. I was watching cultural transmission in full force—adults were evidently still teaching children about law, religion, ceremony, land, hunting, language and other aspects of life. Reports I'd heard that the kids didn't go to school and learn English, literacy and maths now seemed less distressing—if their own systems of education were still working, why should they?

I was aware that this was the kind of experience that non-Aboriginal people come to Arnhem Land for: this was the stuff of intercultural awe and the belief many white Australians hold that Aboriginal people are somehow more spiritual than we are. It's true that I was experiencing a real Aboriginal ceremony, but at the same time, the dancing and singing didn't make much sense to me. I was tired and hot, and the men dancing in the dust were not entertaining enough, without any context or meaning, to hold my attention for long. After a couple of hours I got up and walked home through the hot dark night to my flat.

I'd been told that walking at night was safe. When I asked about personal safety, several people said that although domestic violence was prevalent in the Aboriginal community, it was extremely rare for it to cross over into the white community. Problems within the white community were also rare—I supposed because there were so few Balandas that it would be impossible to get away with much. Still, I moved carefully, partly out of city habits, and partly because it was dark and the streets I walked along were empty. I carried a torch as well as my stick, determined not to be afraid, or at least to not let my fear show.

The stick was in case any camp dogs approached. These were the semi-tamed pets that lay around the Aboriginal houses, usually scavenging food rather than being fed. Being warned about them made me anxious, but they were weak enough to reassure me—many of them had lost parts of their fur, and most of them were thin and downcast, and would run if you threatened them. If a dog approached, raising the stick and yelling was usually enough to deter them. The yell was distinctive—a loud PSHHHHAAAA that sent them running.

When I walked past the basketball courts Aboriginal kids called out to me, 'Hello! Whatsyourname?' I was encouraged by their friendliness.

Back at home, I made dinner and then went to bed after setting the alarm: life's ordinary rhythms persist even with the sound of clapsticks outside your lounge room window.

༖ ༓

I spent most of my first weekend in Maningrida at home alone, continuing to clean out the flat. And I wrote up my first 'bush order' for Coles in Darwin. I needed to fax it to them on Tuesday for delivery on the following Thursday's barge. This meant working out what I would need in two weeks' time, and how much of it I would need to last until the next order came in. I was ordering in bulk: six large cans of tomatoes, a few kilograms of flour, eight cartons of milk, frozen . . . there was an echo of the pioneers ordering supplies in bulk in this experience. Like them, we needed to plan ahead and live out of our store cupboards and keep the bugs out of our food, although now the store cupboard was accompanied by the freezer.

I wasn't going to be by myself all weekend though: I had two dates. Sam, who had come into my office to look at our library, had invited me to a barbecue at her place on Sunday evening with another nurse, Kath, and her husband. I was excited about meeting some more people. I didn't feel any great connection with Sam, but she was friendly, and it was worth a try. And on Sunday afternoon, Alice and Mal had organised a trip to the rangers' station, about a twenty-minute drive from town. The rangers' program sounded a bit like National Park rangers—the slogan was 'caring for country'. It was run as part of the Community Development and Employment Project and was particularly successful. It aimed to get people looking after their land in a coordinated way, as well as using it for economic development.

The rangers' station was at a place called Djingkarr, which was also an outstation for some Gurrgoni families. There were about four houses in the bush, and then the rangers' buildings set in cleared land. One of the houses was for the Balanda who coordinated the rangers' program. The other buildings were for meetings and lessons, with basic accommodation for visiting lecturers and researchers. The rangers were doing a course in resource management run out of the Northern Territory University and lecturers came out to run units of study a few times each year.

Djingkarr was strikingly different to Maningrida. There was almost no rubbish strewn on the ground, and the houses were newer and better cared for than those in town. It happened that there was no-one else there, so we were free to wander around and explore. It was located on a ridge, with a spectacular view of the Liverpool River valley below. There was a smoky haze in the distance—Dry Season was burn-off time, and there were always fires going at this time of year, either deliberately lit to keep the bush under control, or spontaneous fires that burnt through the country. Although this continuous burning meant that bushfires were not a problem, I brought the spectre of fire danger up from the south with me, and had to remind myself that these fires were not something to be feared.

We drove back to Maningrida as the sun was starting to set, catching the now-familiar campfire smell on the breeze as we reached the town. Alice invited me to join them for dinner, but I was going to Sam's barbecue.

Sam lived in one of four small flats down the road from Alice and Mal's house. I walked into the large, dusty garden, bare except for a few trees, and saw that the flats were like most dwellings in the town—plain fibro, slightly worn out. It was only when I turned around that I realised we were right across the road from the rivermouth, which was lit up by a spectacular sunset. It was the most open, beautiful and peaceful vista I'd seen in the town.

Sam's colleague Kath and Kath's husband, Jerry, seemed nice, and at first we were all friendly. He was a mechanic working for the Maningrida council; they had been in town for a few months. But when we got beyond pleasantries, the conversation became strained.

'You can have an alright time here,' Jerry said, 'as long as you don't have to mix with the locals.' I didn't know what to say—I was here because of the locals. Given their attitude, I wondered why they had come to Maningrida.

'It's a good way to make money,' they explained. 'You get paid well, and Kath gets a remote living allowance on top of her wage, and it's cheap to live here. We plan to save for a few months and then move on.'

It had never occurred to me that someone would come here for this reason—it was only when I arrived that I found out exactly what my salary would be, and that the rent on my flat was only $30 per fortnight.

We tried to find something we could all talk about. Kakadu National Park seemed like a safe topic—they had both been there, and Sam had worked as a ranger before moving to Maningrida. But then Jerry started abusing the protestors at the

Jabiluka uranium mine in the park, including the traditional Aboriginal owners of the site. I defended them, and soon the conversation evaporated.

As soon as I could, I came up with a polite excuse and left. I felt sorry for Sam, who had been quiet and, I thought, a bit embarrassed since Jerry and Kath started to pontificate—but at the same time, I would be wary of accepting an invitation from her again.

I talked about it with Mal the next day, and he told me there was a saying that three kinds of people came to Aboriginal communities: mercenaries, missionaries and misfits. I'd met some mercenaries now. And I'd heard about some misfits—the self-appointed caretaker of the airport who had Munchausen's Syndrome came to mind. We were the modern-day missionaries, I supposed. I felt outnumbered.

Three

We stood on the art centre's verandah and watched as an unseasonally full cloud scattered drops over Maningrida.

'This never happens,' said Don, a visiting anthropologist. It was a freak fall of rain, like a message from home, a friendly wink interrupting the unending string of identical sunny days I'd experienced for the previous fortnight. It went after a few minutes, but left the air soaked in its memory, and in my memory of Melbourne.

The next day Don would tell me that the An-barra people he was working with had said that the rain came to scold them for taking so long to organise the funeral of an old man due to be buried. There had been some bickering about where the funeral would take place, but the rain prompted resolution and cooperation.

Don was in Maningrida for a few weeks to work with Tammy, a shortish, plump An-barra woman with a quietly confident demeanour. Researchers like Don used the culture office as a base—they emailed from our computers, used our telephones and came in to talk about how their work was going, and to enjoy some Balanda social contact.

The transient population of Alice and Mal's friends had left the community, but now I moved among another temporary group: academics from the south who flocked to Arnhem Land from June to August, when the weather is perfect every day. In my third week in Maningrida, I found myself at the kind of dinner that can happen in Aboriginal communities. Don was the host and had invited various white academics and some members of the An-barra family who had supplied them all with 'data' for three generations. Brian, an anthropologist, had first come to Maningrida in the 1950s, when the town was just established, and he had been in touch with this family ever since. Tammy's father had known Brian most of his adult life; in fact, she had been named after Brian's wife. I never saw her without her four-year-old niece, Bobette, who had wild, straggly hair and a big smile. They were at the dinner, along with Tammy's husband, Joseph, a large, silent man with tightly curled black hair cut very short. I was brand new, feeling as awkward with the distinguished white academics who knew a lot about Aboriginal culture and language as I did with the An-barra family.

After dinner, Don put on a documentary that had been made in the 1970s. It focused on Tammy's father and a big ceremony taking place on the bank of the Blythe River. After a while I became more fascinated by watching Tammy, Joseph and Bobette watching the film than by the film itself. For them, it was like a home movie: they knew, or at least were related to, nearly everyone in the film. The events taking place were familiar to them, even though they hadn't been there in 1979. They weren't watching it to learn, or to see what happened next, as I was, but for the same reasons Balandas dig out old photos and look at them, or retell stories about things that happened years ago: for the pleasure in remembering. The family's first language was a dialect of Burarra called Gidginarliya. Although Tammy's English was good, and Joseph's was reasonable, Bobette spoke only a few words.

This was an anthropological film, aimed at Balandas, with a voiceover in English and any Gidginarliya subtitled for English-speaking viewers. It explained An-barra culture to a non-An-barra audience. But the An-barra were riveted. I watched the adults explaining the film to Bobette. I tried to eavesdrop, but their own voiceover, of course, was in their own language. A few times Tammy turned to me and proudly pointed out her relationship to the people on screen: that's my mother; that's my father.

Many Aboriginal cultures have taboos against saying the name of a dead person, or having their photograph on display. Around Maningrida there were photos with people cut out of them, and posters with squares removed. I had heard stories of Aboriginal people coming up with elaborate circumlocutions to avoid saying the name of the recently deceased—'that woman Betty, her cousin Fred, well, his father's brother's child'. In English they were usually referred to with a vague 'you know, that old man'. And yet, Tammy was delighted by the images of her deceased mother, claiming the woman on the television proudly as her kin. This might have been because a long enough time had passed since the death. Or it might have been one of the results of Tammy's relationship with the researchers. This family was a bit like reality television subjects, constantly scrutinised and recorded. What would it be like to be someone who had never known a time without the earnest interrogations of anthropologists, assured nearly every Dry Season by visitors from the south that you were worthy of study? For Tammy's generation, and for Bobette, this had always been a part of life. They had shared their culture and language with these outsiders; but what had they taken from the Balandas in return?

~ ~

On the day of the flash of rain, I kept the door to my office closed to trap the conditioned air. I sat in there alone for hours at a time, working on the computer, which was the lifeblood of the centre. Occasionally, I invented an excuse to get up and go out to the warehouse.

This was a huge room in the middle of the centre, tall, vast, uninsulated and unairconditioned. The floor was concrete, and the walls were grubby with years of hand imprints and dust. It trapped the heat on the hottest and most humid days, but mostly its climate was the same as the weather outside, which breezed in through a wide-open roller-door on one wall. There were shelves of baskets and bags in one corner, and sculptures lined up in rows down one side. Bark paintings were either stacked against the walls or arranged on trolleys that looked like giant toast racks.

Elroy sat in the middle of all of this, making a cardboard box to pack a bark painting for freight. He was the centre's longest serving worker. While most of the other workers came and went after a few weeks, Elroy always came back. He wore threadbare t-shirts and old shorts, and had bare feet, like most of the Aboriginal men in town, but he also wore a cap pulled low on his forehead. I had heard him speak English in sentences slowed down by uncertainty, but I had also heard him speak his own language, Djinang, in fluent bursts. I greeted him with 'Manymak?' ('Good?'). 'Yo, manymak,' he replied. That was as far as our conversations had progressed.

A truck was pulling up outside, with people spilling out of it, half a dozen adults and several kids. Anyone big enough to carry an artwork was taking a sculpture or a bark painting wrapped in an old sheet or blanket out of the car. The centre had a policy of buying every piece of art that was brought in, regardless of its quality, as a way of nurturing younger artists, and also supporting the cultural practices of painting on bark, sculpting and weaving. At the same time, only art done in traditional materials would be bought—ochre on bark, rather than acrylic or oil paint on canvas or paper. We supported traditional culture, as well as commercial art production.

I followed the group through to the office to watch as they unwrapped the work for sale. The family was dressed simply, in faded cotton t-shirts, shorts and shirts. The women wore 'zippy dresses', cotton, knee-length, sleeveless, A-line garments with a long zip down the front, sold at the Maningrida shop in a range of bright floral prints. No-one was wearing shoes. The kids were staring at Alice and me, giggling. I smiled at them, feeling shy, and smiled quickly at the adults as well.

Alice greeted everyone: 'Hi Albert! Hi Flora! Hello girls!' She looked at the newest baby, cradled in Flora's arms, and said 'What's this little one's name?'

'Fredelle.'

'Fredelle, aren't you beautiful! Aren't you gorgeous!'

And then it was down to business. While I was admiring a bark painting and two wooden sculptures of spirit figures, Alice was calculating how much to pay for them, based on the prices these artists usually commanded, and the quality of the work. She introduced me to the young man who was the family's main artist, and explained that I would now be writing the docos for the paintings.

'She might humbug you for a story, Albert!' she said.

We all laughed and then Albert finished the conversation with, 'Ma, bony,' ('OK, that's enough.'). The family tumbled out of the office, probably off to the shop for supplies, before heading back to their outstation.

'This is Albert's usual goanna painting,' Alice explained to me. 'The story should already be in the database.' Artists all painted their Dreamings, so each one was limited to a few topics. This meant that we already had the 'story' or cultural explanation for a lot of the work that was brought in. Often, all I needed to do was find an old documentation in the database, then copy and paste it into a new record, fill in the artist's details, print it out and sign the authentication. It was when we didn't have the story, or we only had part of it, that I needed to interview the artist to get the details.

Back in the warehouse, Elroy was having a cup of tea. Because his English was limited, and he could read and write only a few words, there weren't many jobs that he could do. This was true of most of the workers who came to the centre. I was beginning to suspect that boredom with the endless, mundane packing and cleaning might be part of why so many of them only lasted a couple of weeks, rather than their proffered excuses of ceremonial commitments or returning to their country.

This time, Elroy got in first. 'Manymak?'

'Yo, manymak,' I replied.

❧ ❧

The next night, I met one of my neighbours. It was a Saturday, and I had spent the afternoon dismantling Simon's bookshelves and trying to remove years of dust from them. Terry came over as the sun was setting, and I had just finished with the shelves. His huge belly was bursting out of his old blue Bonds singlet, and his hair was long and shaggy.

'Hello,' he said. 'I live in that yellow house.'

I had seen him sitting outside, across the road from the museum, nearly every day.

'Oh, hi, I'm Mary Ellen. I'm working at the art centre.'

He got straight to the point.

'Um, you got any mozzie coil? That shop closed, and we got no mozzie coil. I bring back tomorrow.'

I gave him a few mozzie coils and he left.

A sense of routine was starting to emerge. On weekdays I got up, had breakfast, walked the two minutes to work, spent the morning in my office, came home for lunch, spent the afternoon in my office and then came home late in the afternoon. In the evenings and on weekends I wrote in my diary, talked to friends on the phone, sent emails, made dinner and read books.

At work, I had occasional interactions with Alice, and those fleeting moments with Elroy. I met other Balandas in Bawinanga from time to time, but we rarely spoke beyond the few words needed for introductions. In the first two weeks, I spent some evenings with Alice and Mal and their friends, and when they left, I socialised with visiting researchers. But the visitors and researchers were only around briefly; there was no time to form a real friendship. Instead, I worked on keeping up my friendships with people in Melbourne and Sydney, trying to translate my Maningrida experiences for them, or talking about their lives, which I could imagine and relate to much more than they could imagine and relate to Maningrida. For most of the time, I was simply alone.

Having spent most of my first three weeks with people who would be gone again the following week, I was excited to be invited out for a drink after work by a couple who lived in town. Ron was the accountant at Bawinanga, and Sue was a teacher. We sat on their verandah and set about getting to know each other. They had been in Maningrida for about six months. Sue had short brown hair and was friendly and direct. Ron was relatively short, with a wide round face, quick to laugh or make a joke.

In a supposedly dry community, it seemed strange to be invited over for a drink. In fact, Maningrida was semi-dry: beer in cans came into town every second week, but wine, spirits and beer in bottles were not allowed. You could apply for a beer permit through the council and, until recently, Balandas had been able to apply for a special wine permit as well. I was shocked by this double standard—it seemed so blatantly racist. However, when challenged, Balandas always pointed out that the entirely Aboriginal town council had made the law, and that both white and black were happy with it. The community made the laws to protect itself from alcohol abuse—and they didn't really care what the Balandas drank, as long as we were discreet about it, and it didn't spill over into their community. I was still uncomfortable with it, thinking that surely the principled thing to do would be to just drink beer as the Aboriginal people did. But I was struck by the fact that Balandas were absolutely not prepared to give up wine and spirits while living in a place where they were supposedly prohibited. Every Balanda social event I went to in Maningrida featured contraband grog.

The system was designed to allow alcohol, so that Aboriginal people didn't move somewhere else in search of it, but to contain its effects by allowing it in only fortnightly, and in regulated amounts. The beer came into town every second Thursday, locked in a special container on the barge. It then sat under a stand of mango trees until the following Saturday, when the police handed it out to its owners at 8.30 am. Most Balandas took their beer home and stored it, putting a six-pack in the fridge. But most Aboriginal people started drinking right away, so that by late morning, the town was full of drunk people, yelling, fighting, partying, staggering. 'Wet' weekends had a particular character, very different to 'dry' weekends. The whole town operated around this system: the shop was open for two hours on dry Saturdays, but not at all on wet weekends; in football season, the wet Saturday's games were played on Thursday; and it was accepted that fewer people would come to work on the Monday after a wet weekend.

For Balandas, wet weekends also meant humbug. 'Humbug' meant 'hassle', and the word could be used in a friendly way—

'Can I humbug you for your car?'—but also to refer to serious harassment. Because Balandas had all of the jobs that controlled money, we were often seen by Aboriginal people as resources. The community did not necessarily distinguish between the money given to it by the government, and administered by Balandas, and the personal money that individual Balandas had. Nor did they always see a difference between the services Balandas provided as part of their jobs and personal favours. On wet weekends, these distinctions blurred even more: drunk people would turn up at Balanda houses wanting money for gambling, or a lift to their outstation, or more grog, or just company. The humbug could be loud and relentless, so that the worst affected Balandas either got out of town, or spent most of the day behind closed doors. One Balanda would take to his bathroom, the only room in his house without windows, and spend a few hours reading old copies of the *Bulletin*.

I spent most wet Saturdays in my flat. Terry's house was loud and rowdy some afternoons, and often I would look up at the sound of a car and see the police or an ambulance driving by. If I was invited to Alice and Mal's place they would come and collect me in their car, so I wouldn't have to walk through town. But mostly, wet Saturdays were much like other weekends for me.

The worst of it came on Mondays, when I would hear about the weekend's violence in the camps. The Balandas would talk about which brawl or domestic violence the clinic staff had been

called out to. In the past, the women's centre had operated as a
shelter that women could lock themselves into for the day if they
needed to. Now, many of them tried to go out bush for the day,
returning at sunset when the hangovers were setting in.

∽ ∾

I discovered what humbug meant first-hand when Terry came
back the following Wednesday and asked to borrow $20.

'Tomorrow I give back to you'.

I suspected it was unlikely that I would get the money back.
But then again, I didn't know for sure. Every Balanda in
Maningrida had a story about being humbugged for money. This
was my first time, so I handed over the $20. Archie had told me
that Terry had borrowed $20 from him twice, and paid it back
both times. He had then borrowed $50 and a year later was still
assuring Archie he would pay it back one day. I was interested
to see how this would turn out.

∽ ∾

One wet Saturday I was invited to spend the day on the Blythe
River. Thelma, a Burarra woman who worked with Mal at the
JET Centre, and a couple of her friends, wanted to be out of town
for the day. They had arranged a trip with Ron and Sue, who
got a day out on Thelma's country in exchange for providing the
transport.

Thelma's husband, Tommy, came along as well, driving with a Balanda called Dan, who was in town to work on a revegetation project. Tommy was one of the rangers. Sue told me that both Tommy and Thelma were very good at dealing with Balandas. They spoke English fluently—Thelma was training to become a Burarra–English interpreter through Batchelor University—and they knew enough about our culture to know what made us comfortable and what we had trouble coping with.

To get to the Blythe, we drove out across the floodplain in two four-wheel drives. I was in with Ron and Sue and the 'ladies' (this seemed to be the only word in Aboriginal English for 'women', so it didn't have the connotations of refinement that it usually carries). The floodplain was huge and flat, with great stretches of mud that had dried and cracked, but seemed stable enough for us to drive on. We had no idea where we were, but Thelma gave directions, keeping us well clear of the thin swirl of water that wound across the mud, and the soft ground surrounding it. We reached a mangrove swamp, where we stopped for the women and kids to get out—they would spend the day digging for mud mussels—and then Tommy took us on to the river.

When we got to the mouth of the Blythe we met a friend of Tommy's called Kenny, who was warm and friendly and spoke English well. I recognised him from the Bawinanga office; he was one of the building trainees. He put a billy on the fire to make tea for us, and checked that we were all comfortable and had what we needed. Tammy, who I'd met at the anthropologists' dinner, was fishing nearby with a handline, swinging it above her head like a lasso so that it gained momentum before she hurled it out into the water, then dragged it back into shore. She kept going, a seemingly effortless rhythm in her work, and before long she had caught three snapper for lunch.

The weather was warm and sunny, like every other Dry Season day. A breeze came in across the water. We sat around the fire, making conversation and drinking black tea. Kenny pointed out the two crocodiles sunning themselves on the opposite bank. The men headed down the beach to fish in thigh-deep water, Ron relying on Tommy and Kenny to spot any crocodiles in time.

Sue and I went for a walk, both of us too afraid of crocodiles to go fishing, and then I went to talk to Tammy. We were friendly towards each other, but we had to work hard to produce some stilted chat. It wasn't just the language difficulty, because Tammy's English was relatively good. It was knowing what to say and how to say it. Still, we managed a little conversation, mostly in smiles and nods, mainly referring to the children playing in the shallows.

Later, back at the mangrove swamp, Kenny and Tommy presided over the fire and the conversation in fluent English— and fluent Balanda. I saw what Sue had meant about them understanding us, and I was conscious of my own inexperience in their culture, and in communicating across cultural differences. The ladies made the tea, and then Kenny made sure that everyone had some mud crab, mud mussels and barramundi. We ate it all straight off the fire, peeling the ash-coated skin off the fish, and smashing the crab shells with a rock or a hammer. Everyone was excited by the food, the kids demanding more, the women eating off to one side. The mud mussels were considered a delicacy, so I was disappointed to find them small and tough, tasting slightly muddy.

Tommy entertained us with stories of his travels. One story was about a trip to Japan, which came about when some Japanese researchers who visited Maningrida every year got funding for a reciprocal visit. These were the researchers who had recreated an Arnhem Land outstation in their museum. To make it an exact replica, they offered to pay for 'authentic outstation rubbish' to cover the ground. Aboriginal people came to the art centre for weeks after the offer had run out with bags of rubbish, expecting to be paid for it.

We drove home across the floodplains as dusk claimed them for the night. Thelma and the other women in the back seat tried to teach Sue and me some Burarra, howling with laughter as we mangled the simplest words. We resolved to try and learn some more, but it was rare to have the opportunity to sit with someone like Thelma, without being aware that she had many better things to do than teach a Balanda her language.

I felt content after a day that had been much easier than most of my days in Maningrida. I felt the privilege of being on Kenny, Tommy and Thelma's land with them, and being shown their country and some of their customs. The landscape was spectacular—it brought to mind documentaries that I had seen about Africa—and I was impressed by the people who lived in it and had cared for it for such a long time.

As we reached the town, the wet weekend cast a shadow over my contentment. We dropped Thelma and her friends off in the middle of Side Camp, where there was lots of noise, drunks staggering around and men yelling at each other with spears in their hands. We were safely sealed in the four-wheel drive, on our way to our Balanda houses—we could only hope that the atmosphere of menace and violence would ebb as the hangovers set in.

∽ ∾

I was disappointed by the separation between black and white in Maningrida. It often didn't feel like one community, but rather two different communities living in the same place.

The division wasn't one of animosity, just of foreignness. It was hard to find many similarities in the ways we lived. Before I arrived I might have imagined that I'd make friends with Aboriginal people and we'd drink cups of tea and chat, as I did with Balanda friends. But they drank tea made on an open fire outside while sitting in the dust. I drank tea made in a pot with water boiled in an electric kettle, and I sat in a chair at a table to drink it. I could drink billy tea while sitting in the dust, or on the beach at the Blythe rivermouth. And Aboriginal people could drink Balanda tea and sit in a chair to do it, as Elroy did at work. It was just that we were each disposed to our own way, and needed to make an effort to do it the other way.

I also saw the differences in my interactions with Aboriginal and non-Aboriginal people. With Aboriginal people my mind prickled with an awareness of how little I knew of their language and culture. I crept into these conversations, slowly laying down a tentative friendliness. I did not want to make demands on them, or inadvertently do something offensive.

I went into conversations with other Balandas with more confidence, oblivious at first to how different their subcultures were to mine. Before I understood that white people in Maningrida belonged to different tribes and rarely strayed out of them, I thought of most of them as potential friends. We shared a language and I assumed we might share jokes or experiences or views. I ended up tentative with everyone, with white people, trying not to sound too urban, too southern, too green, and with Aboriginal people like Tammy, Elroy and Jimmy, trying not to impose, or take up too much space on their land. I remember conversations that progressed like a balloon deflating. I learnt to think about my words before I spoke them. I learnt how to stay quiet, and how to swallow my thoughts.

As I got to know Archie more, I felt the now-familiar carefulness fall down like a curtain over my side of the conversation. And yet he was friendly, dropping in to the culture office to see how I was going, and passing on an invitation to join Ron and Sue on their boat on the weekend. But he was also the archetypal 'other Balanda'. He had lived in Aboriginal communities since the late 1970s, drawn to them at a time when Labor Prime Minister Gough Whitlam was handing land back to its traditional owners. Archie was one of a cohort of idealistic white men who laid the foundations of self-determination in Maningrida: he helped to establish Bawinanga, and was still there many years later. He had the Territorian's contempt for what they called 'down south', a contempt that I was coming to know well. It would tint my conversations with these people, mostly older men, and I would see it and try to sound less 'southern', less inexperienced—as well as less young, and less like a woman. I would only realise how badly I had failed in this months later when I walked into Archie's office with a question about ATSIC and he told me he and the visiting auditor were having a terrible week, and then asked me to entertain them and divert them. Being patronised would become a way of life. But for now, I was keen to fit in and to learn, and grateful to be invited out on the boat.

☙ ❧

Being on the boat was like being suspended between sea and sky: two blue domains surrounded us.

Ron, Sue, Archie and I 'camped' under a pandanus tree near Ndjúdda Point, just on the Arafura side of the rivermouth. We went straight out to fish, skimming across the water in the boat holding handlines that trailed out behind us. A lure flickered on the end of the line, and when you felt a tug you knew that a fish had been fooled by its shiny trickery. We took a break to clamber over a reef that had been exposed by the low tide. It was covered with oysters, and I learnt how to prise them off with a rock and a screwdriver. They were the freshest I'd ever eaten, tasting strongly of the sea, although much smaller than oysters I'd had in the city. Back on the water, I was told that it was a slow day, but eventually Ron pulled in a fish, and we went back to the shore for lunch. While the fish was on the fire, Archie went down to the rockpools on the shoreline with a pronged stick to hunt for mud crabs. Having expected to eat sandwiches and take home a fish if we were lucky, I was amazed to be feasting on a lunch of oysters, fresh fish in bread with lime juice, and mud crab.

While we were sitting around the fire after lunch, the talk turned to the town and its people. Archie spoke from his experience: he had stories going back fifteen years, so there was a depth of history behind his observations and analysis that was impressive. But some of his stories articulated a disillusionment I found confronting: if a person with that much experience was downcast about the situation in Maningrida, then what good could any of us really do? I felt like a novice, and didn't say much. I learnt from the conversation that nearly all of the full-time jobs in Bawinanga, and the other organisations in town, were filled by Balandas. Aboriginal people worked almost exclusively in CDEP jobs, which were part-time and almost always low in responsibility. Archie told stories from when he first came to the community, and worked alongside men who planned to take the reins of the organisation from him when they had learnt enough. But this was the tangible side of the statistics that I had heard so many times in the city about the life expectancy of Aboriginal people: the men Archie worked with in the 1980s all died too young to take his place. Now he looked at their sons and daughters and saw unmotivated men and women who hadn't gone to school or, if they had, didn't want to continue the work of their fathers.

Talk turned to Tommy and Thelma, and we told Archie about our day out with them and Kenny the previous weekend.

'Kenny Walker?' Archie said with a sneer. And then came the story. Kenny had spent a few years in jail for sexually assaulting his daughter. His first wife was a Balanda, and she refused to just put up with what Aboriginal women put up with all the time so she pressed charges to protect their daughter. She had not been seen in the town since.

My jaw dropped. Kenny was one of the most 'successful' Aboriginal people I'd met in Maningrida. He was warm and friendly, and had worked as a building trainee for several years. He and Thelma and Tommy had shown that it was possible to live to some extent in both cultures at once, and so to me they symbolised a kind of hope for the whole town. Now I thought he stank, and I didn't know what I'd do when I saw him next. For the others, a story like this was such an everyday part of life that it was stitched into the comments on the weather and how Sue and Ron's children were going. There was no time for shock and revulsion. I closed my mouth and the conversation moved on.

∽ ∾

I was in awe of the way Alice seemed to communicate so easily with Aboriginal people, adopting the Aboriginal English that I was still amazed by. Still unsure how to find my way through the *ims* and *thats* and omissions that seemed to flavour everyday interactions, I spent a lot of time peering into other people's conversations. Eventually, I had to interview an artist without Alice's help, to ask questions and to try to emulate the sounds of an unfamiliar language. I met Lindy, a thin, quiet sixteen-year-old who spoke Kune. She had a childlike shyness and awkwardness, and would be regarded as a kid in my culture. But, like many of the Aboriginal girls her age in Maningrida, she was married to a man about ten years older, and was a mother already. Her screen print was brown and green, a depiction of the rock country that belonged to her family. I drew a sketch of the print in my notebook and began to ask her what all the different things were. She named the river, the rocks, the grass and the plants in her own language and in English, speaking so softly that I had to lean in to hear her words. I repeated what she said and watched smiles flit across her face as I got nearly every word wrong. I grappled with the sounds of Kune—the 'ng' from the end of song turned up to begin a word; there was an 'l' like an English 'l', and then another 'l' as well, curled up with an 'r', and I struggled to hear which was which, and found it nearly impossible to repeat them. I concentrated so much on these closely clustered sounds that often I missed the vowels altogether, shuffling the os and as and is around, inadvertently creating words of my own.

Lindy was patient and polite—I would only realise how polite she had been with me later, when I looked up my transcriptions in the dictionary. My English-speaker's ears had misheard her words so thoroughly that she wouldn't have recognised her own language in what I had written down. I had to resort to looking up 'river' and 'rock' in the English part of the dictionary and working back to excavate the Kune word from the strange string of letters on my page.

Underneath my conversation with Lindy, I could almost hear my mind humming with its unrelenting analysis of the situation. Part of me was preoccupied with politics, race relations and post-colonialism, trying to see my behaviour through the analytical lens I had brought with me from Melbourne. Everything I knew about Aboriginal oppression and dispossession and marginalisation tugged at my words and actions. Is this process appropriate? Am I behaving well? After two centuries of Balandas recording Aboriginal people, am I adding to the weight of research that controlled and demeaned them, or is this something different? Is the conversation between a researcher and an informant inherently oppressive? Does calling you a 'teacher' instead of an 'informant' make any difference? I had read somewhere that direct questions are often considered rude in Aboriginal cultures. So how could I find out what her print contained without asking questions?

Lindy laughed at my mistakes and gave me plenty of time and patience. She would be paid when this print sold and, like all of the artists in Maningrida, she knew that part of selling the art was telling its story. I'm sure that our conversation seemed simpler to her than it did to me, and that its impact on me was much greater than its impact on her. Balandas were nothing new to her.

❧ ❧

Two days later, Valerie came into my office surrounded by sisters, cousins, sisters-in-law and a pack of kids. She had been photographed for the weaving book using a fish trap that her mother had made, looking stunning in a bright pink and white dress, standing thigh-deep in water with the trap in the late afternoon sun. She had a beautiful round face, and big eyes and a big mouth, so her smiles were impressive and luminous. She began to explain her print to me, pointing to the three figures and saying, 'That my father; that my brother; that my mother.'

'What are they doing?' I asked.

'Hunting for mud crab and yam.'

'And what's this?' I asked, pointing to a vine.

'Milil.'

'And this one?' indicating the butterflies.

'Merle merle.'

'Melli melli?'

Valerie laughed and then said very loudly and slowly, 'MERLE MERLE!'

'Merle merle?' This time I got it right, to a chorus of 'Yo, yo, merle merle!'

Then Valerie explained more about her print:

'It Dry season, you can see that milil and merle merle, that mean time for mud crab, and yam, really good one.'

After a while she got stuck—in her language, Kuninjku, and in her social universe, you need to know the relationship the person you're talking to has to the person you're talking about so that you can use the right terms for everybody. She giggled after a while as it all got too hard, and then decided to solve the problem by giving me a skin name.

'You can be belinj, like me. That means you are my sister and you call me yabok.' 'OK,' I said.

This was exciting: Without 'skin' you are always an outsider— you almost don't exist. Being 'given skin' is sometimes confused with being adopted into a family, but in Maningrida it was the most basic form of acceptance. It simply gave you a place in the social universe, so that you could be talked to and talked about. We repeated the words a couple of times, and then Valerie flashed through a kinship lesson, explaining my relationships to everyone in the room, and everyone in the print, and how I should address them and refer to them. It all fell straight out of my head, but I held tight to the two words that I knew might help me build a bridge to this woman: 'belinj', a name she had shared with me, and 'yabok', the word to address a sister.

My notes from this conversation were much closer to the words in the dictionary than they had been with Lindy, so I was able to write quite a detailed documentation about what was going on in the print. But even better than this was the simple experience of hanging out and having fun with Valerie—making silly jokes and laughing. Valerie and her family seemed to move in a big tumble of bodies, and I liked it that they had tumbled into my office so I could be part of it for a few minutes.

On my way home that evening I saw Terry. I called out to him and waved. He returned my greeting, but no mention was made of the $20 he'd borrowed two weeks before. I'd known when I'd given it to him that it was unlikely to be paid back, so I didn't mind. But I would now start following the advice of the other Balandas, who said I should explain I had no money if I was asked for another loan.

∽ ∾

I often saw things in Maningrida that reminded me of the 'news stories' that had previously been my source of information about Aboriginal communities. Here, an issue like alcohol abuse was part of everyday life. The fortnightly beer system kept the problem in check, but it also acted as a constant reminder of the dangers. The fortnightly chaos and its sometimes devastating aftermath were as much a part of the complex, rich, diverse, contradictory world I lived in as the beautiful bark paintings, the smell of the campfires, the ceremonies and the geography of the town. Sometimes, as I observed a wet weekend unfurling, I thought, This is what those news stories were about. But the 'issues' were no longer contained by the neat grid of column inches laid out side by side: they had spilled over from the newspapers into my life.

I had always assumed that the statistics I read about Aboriginal life expectancy meant that fifty-five or sixty was the age most Aboriginal people tended to die. But in Maningrida I came to see that it could also mean that some people lived to be very old, and others died very young, and this could average out to an expectancy of middle age. I seldom heard of anyone dying in their forties, for example. However, another headline was wrought into reality as an epidemic of attempted suicides slowly spread through Maningrida. Almost every barge weekend brought a story of a suicide or attempted suicide. They were always young people, and the tragedy came almost always without warning. Some Balandas speculated that the prevalence of ganja in the town could be the cause: before ganja had become so common, suicide was unheard of there. It seemed possible that on the barge weekends, alcohol and ganja combined with some other, indefinable factor in a way that made some young people try to take their own lives.

It was brought home to me one Monday afternoon when I was in the office writing up the documentation for Valerie's print.

Mal told me that Solomon, one of the building trainees, had killed himself on the weekend. Mal was involved in the building apprenticeship scheme, teaching young men basic maths and applying it to jobs like measuring and estimating.

'He came along most of the time, and he was doing very well,' Mal told me. 'There was no sign that anything was wrong.'

Solomon's death was unheralded by warning signs or a history of depression. There didn't seem to be any explanation, aside from the fact that it was a barge weekend.

The Balandas felt his death acutely, partly because he had been more visible to us as a trainee, but also because it seemed to be a particularly bad sign that someone who was involved in a successful apprenticeship, and apparently committed to it, would take his own life. I wondered what hope there was for the scores of young men and women whose days were stretches of boredom broken only by drugs and gambling, who had none of the structure and sense of purpose that a job or traineeship, or any kind of role at all, can bring. But I knew that this could be a peculiarly Balanda kind of sadness—that the people involved in our programs might have been as lost as those involved in not much at all. As Balandas, we were all involved in program delivery; we had all washed in on the tide of government funding and we wanted to make a good contribution. The suicides suggested an epidemic of hopelessness or despair that was deeply upsetting. We did our work conscientiously, and all around us it seemed that things got worse each fortnight, in increments of one life at a time.

Grog did all kinds of damage. Richard, one of our arts workers, died in Darwin, drowned while drunk, or stoned, or both. He was in his late twenties, and had three small children and a history of drinking. I met him once or twice in the whirl of my first days, before he left the art centre, ending up in Darwin on the drinking binge that ended with his death. I didn't feel any personal grief for Richard, but his was the latest in the line of almost weekly deaths, and because I had met him, and briefly shared a workplace with him, he brought the other deaths closer to me. I was sad for all of them, the old people and the histories that were dying with them, the young people and the tragedy of their truncated lives.

The bodies came back to Maningrida in the plane, a sad cargo delivered all too often from Darwin, where they had died or been autopsied, or from Oenpelli, where the closest morgue was. Each funeral lasted a week or more, and in my first Dry Season it seemed that there was a funeral going on somewhere all the time. The house down the road from me hosted one of the funerals, and my neighbours were up late most nights playing the clapsticks and dancing outside my window.

The smoking ceremony became familiar. As soon as somebody died, all the places they were associated with were smoked. When Richard died, the art centre was closed and a group of men came in with burning twigs and leaves. One of the men, his body smeared with white ochre, played the clapsticks and sang a rhythmic, nasal tune while the smoke filled the room. After about ten minutes, they moved on, taking their ritual to the next place that needed it.

ᖴ ᖴ

The next weekend, Ron, Sue, Alice, Mal and I decided to join Don, the anthropologist, at his rock art research camp for a weekend. He had come back to Maningrida to work with a Rembarrnga family on documenting some of the rock art in their country. He was camping for a few weeks with two of the family's sons, Leo and Isaac, at a place called Dugalajarrany in the rock country south-west of Maningrida. We drove for more than two hours in an old landcruiser that bounced over the rutted dirt road to Korlobidahdah, the outstation closest to the site. The 'boys' were spending every evening there, talking about their day's work with an old man called Billie—Leo's father, Isaac's uncle. Billie was the son of a famous artist and patriarch. He knew the meanings behind the rock art on his country, and the more recent images had all been painted by him, his brothers and their father.

Billie greeted us warmly and showed us around the outstation. It struck me immediately that life here was very different to life in the town. Old corrugated iron structures had recently been replaced by mud-brick houses built by Bawinanga, with outside toilets and solar-powered showers. The houses had four bedrooms each, with an indoor–outdoor kitchen—an undercover, fenced-in room, without any walls. Billie's family had the campfire going just outside this kitchen, but in the Wet they would be able to have a fire under the shelter without burning the place down. Korlobidahdah was quiet, with two big families showing off their new houses, and no-one else around.

We admired the vegie garden and the fruit and nut orchard. As well as the inevitable camp dogs and some scrawny cats, there were geese wandering around. Don pointed out some raised platforms with bark rooves. This was where Billie's family had spent the last few Wet Seasons, before their house was built. Metal and wooden poles had been used to make a semi-permanent structure, but the bark cover must have been a lot like the shelters that Billie's grandparents and great-grandparents would have slept in every Wet Season.

We met the rest of the family. Isaac's brother Abraham had just been out hunting with his rifle. He hadn't caught anything so it was not clear what the family would eat that night. Later, Don explained that they were so poor that when the tucker run came out the previous week, they had had to think hard about what to spend their money on. Some of it went on the staples of sugar, flour, powdered milk and tea, but they had to balance buying food with buying bullets for hunting. For them, a wasted bullet was a serious loss. Don's research was funded by the Australian Institute of Aboriginal and Torres Strait Islander Studies, so he would be paying Leo and Isaac for their work, and the food he bought for the three of them would be shared with the family at the outstation. But when this month of luxury was over, they would be back to carefully weighing flour against bullets. Still, we all noticed how much healthier this family looked than the town people, aside from Billie, who was terribly thin and had respiratory and heart problems that kept him at home instead of clambering over rocks with his sons.

There was another difference as well: Billie's wife stayed silent through the visit, sitting a little apart from the group, her head lowered and her face turned away. In Maningrida, women were not so obviously subservient.

We left for the half-hour drive to the camp, driving along tracks and across a creek in the gathering dusk. There were about five rocky outcrops at the site, and although it was dark when we arrived we peered at some of the paintings on them by torchlight. We set up our swags and mozzie domes on a platform of rock where Leo and Isaac said it was least likely that marauding buffalo could attack in the night. A boulder rose above the platform and housed one of the rock art 'galleries' that was being documented, and also a cave in which the bones of a long-deceased relative were laid. It was a somewhat uncanny place to sleep.

The next day Leo, who was seventeen, and Isaac, who was eleven, guided us around the rocks near the campsite and then on to a spot about half an hour's walk away where there were figures and animals painted all over the rocks. Leo was fairly tall and broad, but looked as though he was still growing. He was quiet, confident in what he was doing but awkward in his interactions with us. Isaac was small, thin and energetic, chatting confidently, making jokes, pulling faces and laughing. They both wore the ubiquitous faded t-shirts and shorts and Isaac carried an old, faded plastic soft-drink bottle full of water, tied on a loop of string that he slung over his shoulder. Some of the paintings had been faded by exposure to sun and water; others were on protected rock faces and had been preserved. We found graceful, elongated stick figures, some wearing baskets on their arms, and hand prints that had been made by holding a hand against the rock and blowing a mouthful of white ochre over it. There were kangaroos and the rainbow serpent spirit, as well as a few more recent paintings: a cryptic outline that Don, Isaac and Leo had puzzled over for hours had turned out to be Billie's attempt to draw an aeroplane.

I tried to come up with a Balanda equivalent for how well these young men knew their country, likening Isaac's command of plants and animals to the knowledge of an eleven-year-old who gets straight As at school, and thinking that Leo was the Rembarrnga equivalent of a successful Year 12 student. But it felt different from that. To me, their country was entirely foreign. Hot, dry and capricious—the dusty ground we walked on, with its sparse vegetation and tendency to burn, would be entirely under water during the Wet Season. Climbing was hard work, and I knew that I wouldn't survive out there alone for more than a few hours. But they were entirely at home there, leaping over the rocks as sure-footed as I am on a city street. I realised that what they saw was completely different to what I saw: they could see food, and shelter, and water, while all I could see was the absence of anything familiar and comfortable.

They communicated with each other in Kune, and in a system of hand signals that flickered past my eyes as I watched. At night, Isaac went hunting along the river for prawns and after dinner he sang and played the clapsticks while Leo accompanied him on the didjeridu. Isaac was brainy and charming and confident among foreign adult strangers; he eclipsed his cousin who, although older, was quiet and shy and spoke less English. Nevertheless, it was obvious that these young men knew a lot and were continuously learning more from Billie and others. Although Billie was the expert, they still knew many of the stories about the paintings and were able to recount them for us in articulate English. They knew their country; they knew about hunting; they knew songs and stories and they spoke at least two languages each. I don't know whether either of them had been to school but I doubt that they could read and write. At Dugalajarrany and Korlobidahdah it hardly seemed to matter.

On the way home we stopped to thank Billie for our stay on his country. I felt that I had been shown a whole different side of Aboriginal life and culture, and it made me feel much better about being in Maningrida. I felt more inspired about the language project: I had seen that Leo and Isaac spoke Kune and hardly any Rembarrnga, even though it was their parents' language. There were a couple of strong languages overtaking the smaller languages, and now I saw how our learner's guides and dictionaries could be valuable to these communities.

◦~◦ ◦~◦

The families at Korlobidahdah only came into town when they had to. They had shown me that children growing up in their 'mother-country' or 'father-country' could receive a thorough education from older relatives. But I also knew that aside from the families who divided their time between the town and the bush, increasing numbers of people were staying in town permanently. They were born there, they grew up there and continued to stay when they had children of their own. Many of them spoke Burarra, the language that was coming to dominate in the town. They knew their country, but not as well as Leo and Isaac knew theirs: they learnt less about hunting, religion, ceremony and law than if they had lived on an outstation. In Maningrida itself, there was hardly any bush food available, and because the town was on land owned by the Ḍkurridji clan, other clans couldn't easily conduct ceremonies there.

It was impossible for kids in town to get a proper Aboriginal education. But they didn't go to Balanda school and learn to count and read and write and speak English either. In Maningrida, the jobs that needed education were all done by Balandas, while Aboriginal people depended on welfare. The gap between the two groups seemed increasingly wide, and increasingly permanent.

When this became clear to me, I understood how Balanda education would seem irrelevant to most Aboriginal people.

If I thought of life on the outstations as black, and formal Balanda education as white, then, it seemed to me, people in town were forming a new, murky-grey class. For them, Maningrida must be a pretty boring place. There was a bit of fishing to be had; not much work; football for men during the Wet Season and basketball for anyone during the Dry. Welfare payments provided enough cash to buy food at the store, to gamble and to buy ganja. In a life so boring, gambling and drugs were the only respite.

For many of the kids growing up in this grey town, school was just a place to go to buy food and soft drinks. But mostly, they wandered around all day, waiting until they were old enough to get into drugs and gambling. I heard a constant stream of stories, from Balandas and Aboriginal people, about kids vandalising gardens, overturning rubbish bins, destroying anything that wasn't tied down. Stories of kids as young as seven crying out for ganja. Stories of children going hungry while their parents gambled through the night. The circle of adults with cards and hands flicking was a permanent fixture in certain parts of town; and around it, children leaning against the shoulders of their parents, watching the action.

Korlobidahdah had made me see the deficiencies in the town more clearly. I looked back on the ceremony I had seen in my first week, and it now seemed like a watered-down version of what it ought to have been. Kids dancing in a crude imitation of the adults: Isaac would have known the dance properly and would have outclassed them all. The bottle of coke in the ten-year-old's hand now looked like a symbol of drug addiction, a potent cocktail of caffeine and sugar. Now it reminded me not of a kid having a drink in a globalised community, but of the high rates of diabetes and heart disease in Arnhem Land and places like it, and the early death they caused.

༄ ༅

There was an indigenous language conference in Alice Springs at the end of September, and I decided to go. I hoped that talking to people who ran language programs, and visiting the Institute of Aboriginal Development, where there was a language unit that had produced learners' guides and dictionaries for Central Australian languages, would help me find a way to start the Maningrida project. I could see that I was stymied, partly by inexperience, but also by the philosophical doubts that I had started to have about the work done by Balandas in Maningrida.

I would be away for five days, and I would come back with a plan.

Four

On a Saturday morning in the middle of September I stood on my verandah and thought of high school geography classes: 'Tropical zones have only two seasons, a Wet and a Dry.' The less famous third season had just begun: the Build Up, when the humidity intensified every day until finally the wet came to disperse it. I had been told that the Wet Season was climate melodrama—huge storms every afternoon, a sky full of lights and bangs—but I just couldn't imagine it. Like a lazy person, this air felt too heavy to move. My skin was blooming with sweat all the time. It was the season for mangoes, and finally I understood that such an intense, sticky, sweet fruit could only be incubated in air like this—compressed, hot, moist. From the edge of my verandah I could see the rivermouth, and I looked for sea breezes, but nothing disturbed this overweight air.

It was a grog-free weekend, so I went to the shop. I didn't need anything in particular, but walking to the shop on Saturday

mornings, I could pretend that I lived in a real town. I bought
the previous weekend's *Australian*, which would have come in on
Monday or Tuesday, and some eggs and milk. I looked at the
fruit and vegetables. They were all sealed onto Styrofoam trays
with thick plastic, and carried the smells of rot and intense
refrigeration. They were usually brown, shrivelled or pale—it
was months since I had seen a fresh leafy green vegetable, and
as usual I compensated by buying a tray of flaccid green beans.

Back home, I lay on the couch next to the window, reading
the newspaper. The fan blades whirled and moved the air but
couldn't cool it. Sweat squelched behind my knees and seeped
onto my face and arms. On the verandah, half a dozen different
kinds of insects moved, stunning in their abundance and efficiency.
Green ants rushed along my washing line to get to the grevillia
tree, laden with bright orange flowers full of honey. At night, the
geckoes would emerge, clinging to the roof with their suction-
cap feet, to catch the ants on their slick tongues.

These weekends in the Build Up were empty, long, too hot.
The visitors had stopped for the year, and I was no longer a new
person surrounded by transient researchers and art buyers. I was
living here through the Build Up along with all the other
permanent staff. It was too hot and humid for the effort of
housework. There wasn't much to do but think.

෭ ෨

At the opening dinner of the language conference, I had felt cold for the first time in months—I had forgotten that the temperature drops in the desert at night. I met up with Jane, who I had studied linguistics with at university. She was now working at the Institute of Aboriginal Development (IAD) writing a dictionary of a Central Australian language. She led me to the IAD table. I sat down and looked around. I had expected the conference to be full of Balandas like me who worked for Aboriginal organisations. I was shocked to see that at least ninety per cent of the people there were Aboriginal, and then was instantly ashamed of my reaction.

Most of them were working on their own languages and wanted funding for projects that they were already running as volunteers. Many of them were older women who taught at their grandchildren's schools in the hope that their own languages would not be forgotten in favour of Kriol and English.

On the first morning I heard a panel of Aboriginal people who were running language programs in schools. One of them, Jackie, was in her thirties, articulate and passionate about her work. She taught at an Aboriginal college in Alice Springs. The school community seemed to be driven by their hope that education for kids that came from their own culture might be the answer to drug abuse and dropping out. The school had been badly hit by the Northern Territory government's decision to stop funding bilingual education programs. Jackie spoke mainly about what the school had achieved and why it mattered, and touched on how hard it was to operate without any funding. She was one of those confident, intelligent, gregarious speakers who captivate their audience. She would be a great teacher.

I had lunch with Jane and Dorothy, a teacher who was working on a dictionary of her own language. Every night after work she would get the generator going in her tin-shed house to put in at least an hour on the language work while supervising her daughter's homework. Dorothy was quiet, but self-assured and determined, rather than shy. As she and Jane drifted into a conversation about work, I thought about Jackie, and about the impact that great teachers can have on their students. I wondered who was like that in Maningrida. All of the teachers there were Balandas. They taught alongside Aboriginal teachers, known as 'ATs'. The ATs didn't necessarily have any qualifications; in fact, some of them couldn't read and write. They were nominated by their community and, if they were out bush, it was up to them to run the outstation schools on days when the Balanda teacher was in town or at a different outstation. If they were in the town, they worked at the school alongside the Balanda teacher.

I looked across the room at Jackie, and across the table where Jane and Dorothy were still deep in conversation. This was what I had thought Maningrida would be like: Balandas working with Aboriginal colleagues for Aboriginal bosses. In my three months in Maningrida, my role in the entirely white service industry there had come to seem normal. Now, from the other end of the

Northern Territory, I looked back on the art centre and Bawinanga and I saw them in a new way.

After lunch there was a panel on funding. ATSIC staff members stood up and read prepared speeches about different programs. Words and acronyms washed over us: ATSLIP, FATSIS, Language Access Initiative . . . The audience wanted to know how to get funding for their programs. Some of them had applied unsuccessfully in the past, others didn't know how to apply. When it was time for questions, they stood up and vented their anger at the pale bureaucrats before them. The ATSIC staff knew only the language of bureaucracy, and so they continued to speak of funding years and grant acquittals and local area representatives. It had become a language conference without a lingua franca, and the frustration was palpable.

Jackie stood up and asked about the Language Access Initiative.

'You said there's money there for us, for language,' she said. 'How can we apply?'

Her question shocked me, because I already knew the answer. It was a three-year program. The money for the first two years had already been allocated—that's where the art centre's $190,000 had come from. The third year was on hold: ATSIC had not yet decided whether it would accept new applications, or give the funding to existing applications that had missed out in the first two years.

At some stage, about a year ago, Alice had found out about the LAI and put together a proposal for $1 million. Meanwhile, Jackie and her colleagues, and most of the people in the room, had been unaware of the program. Now, as the staff explained, it was almost certainly too late.

The LAI was a one-off, part of a scheme put together by the government in response to the Stolen Generations report. These language and cultural programs recognised the cultural damage done by the policy of removing children. I was in a room full of faces of every shade of brown, testament to the genetic intermingling that had gone along with colonisation in this part of Australia. There would certainly have been people in the room with me who had been directly affected by the child removal policy, possibly people who had been taken away themselves, or had children taken from them. In Maningrida, the Aboriginal faces were nearly all the same deep, dark, rich shade of nearly-black brown. Intermarriage with Balandas was rare. And because it had always been like this, because there were almost no 'half-castes' in the area, the children had stayed with their families and grown up speaking their own languages.

Jackie was angry. 'We need more money so that we can teach our kids, and you're telling me the government has already spent the language money!' The speakers on the platform had to take whatever was thrown at them, forced to accept the communities' anger on behalf of a system that didn't work. I wondered how often they found themselves in this position.

Nobody went to the workshops that were supposed to end the day. A feeling of helplessness had engulfed the conference.

I spent the evening watching television in my hotel room. The TV in my flat was besieged with snow and static, so I luxuriated in the crisp images and clean sound.

At lunch the next day Jane introduced me to a woman called Agnes. Later, I asked whether she was also working on the dictionary.

'Oh no, Agnes can't speak her language, she speaks Kriol. She's meant to be learning Arrente but she never turns up.'

I remarked that she was very friendly.

'Yeah I suppose so,' Jane said. 'She's sucking up to me because she was meant to come in last week to help with a workshop and she didn't show up.'

Jane went on to explain that Agnes was part of a powerful Alice Springs family who spent a lot of time at the Institute.

'They like to throw their weight around and remind you who's boss.'

'*Are* they your boss?'

'No—a couple of them might be on the management committee, but really they just like to tell whitefellas what to do.'

The afternoon session was an open discussion about language work and what could be done in the future. I noticed that although most of the speakers and people asking questions over the last two days had been women, in this open forum it was the men who spoke. Most of the contributions were rallying cries about keeping language strong and being proud of culture. There was talk of sending a strong message to the government that funding had to be provided. Then Agnes stood up and said that Aboriginal people needed to be recognised for their knowledge.

'We get those white linguists coming in, they learn our language, then they go back to Sydney and Canberra and they get a university degree. We know our language, but we got no degree!'

Others joined in: 'They come here, learn our language, the university says they are a linguist. I know my language, I am an Aboriginal linguist!' 'What about university degrees for us? The whitefella take our language back to Sydney, we get nothing.'

The rhetoric seemed to come out of a tradition of protesting about exploitation. These communities must have had their share of researchers coming in and learning about them and then leaving again. However, there was a nasty edge to this discussion, because in fact all the linguists in the room were working on dictionaries—they weren't just researching PhDs. In most cases the language speakers didn't know how to write a dictionary, or write down the grammar of the language so that it could be taught. Linguists had to do that for them.

Later, Jane explained that it all went back to internal community politics in Alice Springs. 'That family just needs something to be angry about,' she said. 'None of the people we work with feel that way. Dorothy doesn't feel like that, and she knows much more about dictionaries and grammar than that mob.'

It was yet another side to the Aboriginal communities in and around Alice Springs. There, Aboriginal people seemed both much better off and much worse off than the community in Maningrida. In Alice Springs, their cultures and languages had been damaged by Balanda interference, and they were struggling with these losses as well as acute social problems. But the same people were more autonomous and empowered than most of the Aboriginal people in Maningrida, holding many of the jobs with responsibility, and initiating and carrying out their own projects. At the same time, politics and power struggles were threaded through all of these Aboriginal organisations.

I went back to Maningrida with a head full of contradictions, and a growing sense that the way things were in Maningrida was not the only way things could be.

ೲ ೲ

Monday morning was always busy at the art centre, with people selling what they had painted or made over the weekend. On this particular Monday, I was faxing documentations and artist CVs to a private gallery in Melbourne, which was about to have an exhibition of Maningrida work. I had used my best university-educated, authoritative English to write these documents, as I did in all of my writing for the art centre—brochures, journals, books, information requests and the centre's website. Many of the words I wrote appeared alongside the phrase 'Maningrida Arts and Culture is a community-based arts organisation'. Unlike our new Macintosh computers and our databases, our fax machine was the kind of thing you would expect to find in a community organisation—ancient, temperamental and slow. As I nursed each page through its grinding mechanism, I waited anxiously to see a red dot on its reverse side—the sign that it had gone through. These elusive red dots would only appear about half the time.

As I faxed, I could hear Alice on the phone to the gallery owner. She was discussing the prices for the exhibition, a complex negotiation that tried to keep the prices low enough so that the work would sell, but not so low that the artist's reputation would be cheapened. She was also negotiating the inclusion of some new artists, but the gallery owner wasn't keen. She wanted only established artists, because she knew that their work would sell. Beck, our admin assistant, had photographed the work, scanned the images in to the computer and then emailed them to the gallery.

I went out to the warehouse to find Beck showing Ralston and Elroy which paintings needed to be packed up for shipping. Ralston was one of about a dozen Aboriginal men who drifted in and out of work at the art centre under the CDEP scheme. He always seemed to be smiling in the awkward, self-conscious way of an adolescent, and his droopy posture and dragged-along walk added to the effect. In fact, he was no younger than the other workers—just far less comfortable with himself. He would come to the centre and declare that he would be working full-time from now on, stay for two or three days, and then not be seen again for a month.

Maningrida was full of contradictions and insurmountable problems, and the CDEP scheme was its overarching compromise. It was so much a part of life that it became a word rather than an acronym—'cedeepee' to Balandas and some Aboriginal people, 'jiddibby' to other Aboriginal people. Towns with limited employment opportunities could run a cedeepee program, which paid wages that were about the same as the dole, and also gave the community funding for projects that would generate employment. Bawinanga got the money from ATSIC, paid the wages every fortnight and used the extra funding to support projects like the art centre, a mud brick factory and a garbage collection program. People were paid to work in one of the designated projects, and paid extra 'top-up' if they worked for more than the required twenty hours. People who lived full-time on an outstation were paid cedeepee for 'traditional cultural activities'. Although it was an expensive program, it was said to appeal to the government because it got thousands of Aboriginal people off unemployment benefits; and the money that would have otherwise gone to them through the Department of Social Services went through ATSIC, inflating the total annual ATSIC funding that the government could claim. The communities liked the scheme for the extra funding it brought in; in Maningrida, with so many participants, the scheme brought in hundreds of thousands of dollars a year.

Like so many of the initiatives, programs and schemes that brought money into Maningrida, cedeepee seemed like a reasonable idea but could not be made to work. If people like Elroy and Ralston signed on to a cedeepee project in the town, but only went to work some of the time, they would still be paid regardless of whether they had clocked up their twenty hours. And people who were paid for traditional cultural activities could come into town and 'sit down' (do nothing), and still be paid.

Some Aboriginal people got enough top-up to feel that they were earning money; but many others were working twenty hours a week for not much more than the unemployment benefits other people got for doing nothing. Cedeepee didn't give its workers much of a financial reason to go to work—it was no surprise that Ralston was happy to drift between cedeepee and unemployment benefits, or UB, as the dole was called. For many Aboriginal people, cedeepee was just a more complicated form of welfare.

Cedeepee had other problems too. At the art centre, most of the guys—as we referred to the cedeepee workers—couldn't read and write much, though some of them could add and subtract a little. So they spent most of their time cleaning and packing. Occasionally, they treated art for mould and borer or moved it around when they were told to. A couple of times a week they drove art around town, up to the airport or across to the barge when it needed to be shipped away. They always worked under white instruction while the Balanda staff sat at computers and telephones and worked within a different world, a world of

Balanda norms and language and requirements. The more this community art centre achieved, and the more efficient we made it, the less its community could be directly involved, except as manual labour.

Many of the guys found a reason to move on after a few weeks—it could be ceremony, boredom, love, culture, gambling, country or family. This made it difficult to give them more responsible jobs. None of the agencies wanted to be left with no-one to do the work when a ceremony came up, or the worker decided to go back to their country.

It was now 10.30, and in the Bawinanga office, where I had gone to post the original documentations, Kelvin was still sorting the mail that he had collected from the 9 am flight. Morris and Alan were chatting at the big table in the centre of the room.

There was a brief pause in the flow of Burarra as they greeted me: 'Hallo, gun-mala?' ('good?')

'Yo, gun-mala.' There was never much activity here, a contrast to the surrounding offices, in which Balandas tapped on computer keyboards or hunched over pieces of paper full of figures and lists and regulations.

I walked into Jenny's office to get the envelopes and stamps I needed. Jenny was about fifty, and she and her husband had worked in several Aboriginal communities over the years. They liked the lifestyle—they went out fishing on their boat every weekend, and were happy having the quiet life that remote communities offered.

BALANDA

'Kelvin's meant to be helping me with this but he's been going on that mail all morning,' she said.

It was rare for Jenny to be flustered, but I could see that there were invoices and receipts all over her desk, so I didn't stop for a chat.

I was never quite sure who of the ten or so Aboriginal people who hung out in the Bawinanga office were cedeepee workers, and who were elected committee members. Bawinanga was structured so that its members elected an executive committee, which then directed the organisation, with staff carrying out the directions. In practice, the Aboriginal committee didn't have the education needed to grapple with the bureaucracy that made Bawinanga tick, so the Balanda staff ran the organisation, and reported their activities to the committee. Because it was run by principled Balandas, this system worked well enough in practice but in theory the decisions were supposed to be made by the committee. I had an uneasy sense that if the staff had wanted to embezzle or mismanage the money, the committee would be unlikely to have the skills to know what was going on, or to take steps to stop it.

I walked back through the warehouse. In the office, Alice was now buying baskets from a group of women and Beck was doing the banking. Elroy and Ralston were surrounded by cardboard and bark. I went into my own office, and checked that I had attached the right story to the back of each painting, and that each had a signed certificate of authenticity. I had updated the artists' CVs for the exhibition, making sure that they were formatted to look their best. I had sent copies of everything to the gallery. Now I could close the databases and go back to work on the weaving book.

∽ ∾

I lay on my couch, fans whirling frantically overhead, the phone sweaty in my hand, talking to Shelley, who was in Melbourne, wrapped in a doona, huddling in front of a heater. We had been at uni together, involved in student activism, and we had spent hours in the coffee lounge talking about politics, feminism, post-modernism, gossip and books. We had been so sure of ourselves and our black-and-white political views when we were twenty. Things seemed less clear-cut now, but we still came up with theories about the world, trying to make sense of everything by capturing it in conversation.

We had talked a lot about Aboriginal issues over the years, trying to figure out what we thought, what was right and what ought to be done. We had worked out a framework for understanding Aboriginal issues that was typical of the young, left-wing, social-justice-oriented people we knew.

It was clear to us that because Aboriginal people had been wronged by the white invasion, the Australian government ought to give them as much money as it would take to fix or alleviate the problems that colonisation had caused. The social problems, like domestic violence and alcohol abuse, health problems like

diabetes and heart disease, economic problems, language loss—
all of these should be tackled by government programs, because
we owed it to Aboriginal people. Before I went to Maningrida,
it hadn't occurred to me that 'solutions' that came from the outside
could be so ineffective.

Now I was trying to explain to Shelley that I was worried
by welfare dependency, and by the social problems that it caused.
Unlike in the Balanda world, where unemployment benefits are
intended to be temporary, in Maningrida Aboriginal people know
from experience going back a couple of generations that they
would always be paid welfare. This was not so bad for those
people who still lived most of the time on their land and had
cedeepee as a kind of income augmentation. But for those people
in town who did nothing all day, our welfare system was insidious
and destructive.

'Imagine a suburb of Melbourne,' I said to Shelley, 'with 1500
long-term unemployed people, whose lives were run by a separate
class of salaried workers. It just wouldn't happen.'

Depression can steal motivation and a sense of competence
from its sufferers, and it seemed to me from what I'd seen that
welfare dependence did the same thing. Welfare paid for food,
tobacco and diesel, with enough left over for gambling and ganja,
the only things available to relieve the boredom.

'You've changed,' Shelley remarked. 'Remember what we said
about Anna's stepfather?'

She was right. About five years before, when we were housemates, I had taped some of our conversations for a linguistics project. I could still clearly remember deriding this man because he thought that the problem with Aboriginal people is that they've got a welfare mentality. In 1995, I thought his analysis was ignorant and racist. And now here I was, telling Shelley all about the problems of the Aboriginal welfare mentality in Maningrida, and how it was reinforced by the good intentions of Balandas—including me.

It was true we were there, mainly, in some kind of service of Aboriginal people. Though nearly all of us were staunchly atheist, it was true that in some way we sought atonement for the sins of our fathers. We reiterated the saying about mercenaries, missionaries and misfits. The mercenaries were transient contractors: Ted the concreter, Alan and Bill the Telstra guys, Con and Theo the roofers. Their world was tin and concrete and 'green cans' (VB tinnies), a shanty town of 'dongers', demountables down near the workshops, slightly apart from where the rest of us lived. The misfits didn't form a group: some assimilated into the Balanda community, others lived with an Aboriginal family or entirely on their own. The rest of us were left to the missionary category. Depending on your point of view, you might take this label as a joke—or you might read more into it, and be prompted to wonder what the similarities between you and a missionary really were.

But we weren't there to convert or assimilate. Many of us were there because we thought that Aboriginal cultures were intrinsically worth preserving. By taking on the Balanda aspects of their lives for them, we wanted to protect Aboriginal people from contamination by the dominant culture, leaving them free to continue to live their traditional lives, augmented by the financial support that welfare gave them, and by the benefits of housing, roads, cars and a health clinic. In this way, they could benefit from both systems, taking what they wanted out of our culture, but retaining their own values, language, ceremonies, education and culture.

But I had begun to doubt this analysis since coming back from Alice Springs. I'd started to think that maybe the processes of cultural interaction were more insidious than this: maybe our good intentions were actually wounding them.

Things rarely ran in an Aboriginal way in Maningrida. I had expected to be surrounded by the exotic, but instead I was enmeshed in white bureaucracy, a jungle of Latinate terms like acquit, triplicate and application.

Sometimes I even wondered whether our presence in the community, rather than protecting their culture, was in itself a step towards assimilation. After all, we brought aspects of the dominant culture in with us. I would try to work out whether this was a bad thing, and think myself round in circles. Health care and health education seemed essential, but they could be interpreted as assimilationist: for example, teaching Aboriginal people how to think about food and hygiene in a Balanda way, instead of an Aboriginal way. It seemed to me that the immediate necessity of healthcare was more important than philosophical questions about the imposition of one culture onto another. We had to accept that in some cases, imposing our culture would benefit Aboriginal people. But I had learnt that Balandas would never, ever articulate it in those terms. There was a strong taboo in the white community against being an assimilationist. The whole community was founded on the post-Whitlam ideals of land rights and self-determination. In practice, this meant that covert, unintentional assimilation—such as health care—went unspoken.

We accepted the system that we inherited, and assumed that eventually, with education, Aboriginal people would step into the jobs now done by Balandas. Training was our mantra: every project that sprung up in town had a training component attached to it. Eventually, it seemed that we could get funding for almost anything we wanted to do, as long as we were training Aborigines in it.

Despite these intentions, there was very little crossover between the two cultures, although we lived side by side. It seemed unlikely that Aboriginal people would ever start behaving like Balandas: that they would become literate, acquire a forty-hour per week work ethic and take on responsibility for managing money the Balanda way in the face of family pressure to use that money the Aboriginal way. And why *should* they start acting like Balandas? To them, I imagined we were pale imitations of humans, with no culture or religion or law or understanding of anything that was important. Ceremony is at the core of Aboriginal law and identity and spirituality in Arnhem Land and, judging by our lives in Maningrida, Balandas had no ceremony. We left town for Christmas, and for weddings and funerals. Most of us had left family and friends behind in other parts of the country, and so our big events happened away from Maningrida.

Part of my job was to ask artists to tell me the stories in their paintings, so that I could write them down. Linguists and anthropologists and other researchers came to town every Dry Season with their questions. Cross-cultural communication in effect meant unfurling our ignorance about Aboriginal culture. Reaching out in friendship to Aboriginal people, we would often ask questions in the face of nothing much else to say.

It occurred to me that this probably made them feel sorry for us. It would be logical for them to assume that we had no culture to speak of and so were hungry to devour as much of theirs as we could. Balandas reflected this assumption as well, speaking of themselves as though they were 'culture-less' (bad) and of Aboriginal people as 'culture-rich' (good), rather than seeing two distinct cultures, both with their good and bad qualities, their riches and deficiencies.

So why would Aboriginal people try to be more like Balandas?

∽ ∾

Nevertheless, we worked towards leaving behind a legacy of solid infrastructure that Aboriginal people could use, maintain and run if only they had the will to do it. We turned away from the worst possibility—that to do this they might need to leave their Aboriginality behind. We claimed that with enough training everything would be fine. Everything would be handed over. We would make ourselves redundant.

The 'Aboriginal situation' was a continual topic of conversation among the Balandas. This meant talking about why it was that Aboriginal people didn't send their children to school, didn't accept the training programs they were offered and didn't take on the jobs that we were doing for their community. I felt that they simply didn't need these aspects of our culture, and probably didn't want them. Having avoided some of the worst of what colonisation brought to Aboriginal people, they didn't have the kind of motivating forces that their counterparts in other parts of Australia had. Despite the dilution of culture in the town, most people's languages were flourishing, their children were growing up knowing what they should do for ceremony, their dead were buried the right way, and they knew their land and how it worked.

The reality was that Aboriginal people were making us indispensable: they had no intention of taking on our jobs and worries when there was no earthly need to do so. But I wondered whether the day would come when the government funding was cut, or when for some reason there were no Balandas willing to come to Arnhem Land and do the community's work for it. Most of the Aboriginal people there had never known a time without a benevolent Balanda presence in their lives, and without the flow of government money into their hands.

Five

THE BARGE WAS DUE AT 6.30. I KNEW THAT IT WOULD TAKE A while for the building materials and cars to be taken off, and that I could probably safely get there at 7. The timing was important: too early, and I would need to stand around and wait; too late, and the groceries that had come out of the refrigerated or frozen containers would sit in the sun. I had bamboo blinds coming in on this barge, as well as the usual groceries, so I had arranged to borrow Alice and Mal's truck to go and collect them.

My timing was wrong. I spent half an hour waiting for the food containers to be unloaded, surrounded by clumps of blokes. Plumbers, builders, landscapers, roofers and handymen turned up, their trucks forming a fleet in the dust. They looked down at the dirt and spoke to each other while I waited, alone and conspicuous, leaning on my truck or pretending that I had something to do. When finally the first food container landed, we all surrounded it as a couple of men unloaded the boxes.

I counted the crowd as we waited: nineteen blokes and me. I loaded my truck, doing for myself what these men were doing for their wives, and drove the half-kilometre home. It was 8.30 and already I felt exhausted.

The day turned into another humid, disgruntled afternoon. I went to get a painting from the art office, and Alice introduced me to George, a new worker. He was a stout man, with eyes that disappeared in wrinkles when he smiled, and a hint of stubbornness in the way he tilted his chin up as he talked.

'I'm going to start here on Monday' he told me.

'That all sounds great, George,' Alice said. 'We'll see you on Monday.'

'OK, see you then.'

After he'd gone, Alice explained that George was the son of one of the region's most famous artists, and an artist himself. He seemed very confident and competent.

In the time before he started, we heard more about George. The most striking thing was that so many Balandas had something to say about him. Most of the cedeepee workers came and went quietly, but George was the kind of person who other people notice. We learnt that he used to work at the mud brick factory and ended up practically running it, and that his English was fluent, and he could read and write.

In George's first few days we discovered that he was friendly, talkative and quick to laugh. His English was more fluent than any of the other arts workers—and because he laughed and talked along with the Balanda staff, he opened up a friendly flow between us and the cedeepee staff that was impossible without shared language. Walking through the warehouse now involved a chat, a joke, a quick comment called out across the room. He came in every day, and the art centre became his territory. He worked out what needed to be done each day, and organised the other guys into doing it. Having asked Alice in the morning what had to be packed up, he would have it on the 5 o'clock plane that afternoon.

The official story about the art centre was that it was run by Aboriginal people, but in fact it had been run by Balandas for years. Alice was setting up an artists' committee to at least nominally run the centre. So far, they had met only a couple of times, and could not yet do much beyond listening to Alice's account of what she had been doing, and approving her decisions.

George organised the committee's third meeting. I remembered how in my first week Alice and I had spent a whole afternoon trying to find Nellie. Finding people on outstations was much more complicated—it meant calling a public phone and hoping that the person who answered it could help. You had to follow a trail across language barriers from public phone to public phone until you found the person you were after.

George spent a couple of days on the phone, the air full of Burrara as he tracked people down, organised lifts and confirmed the day and the time. Compared with what a Balanda would have achieved in the same time, it seemed miraculous. On the day of the meeting, everyone was there, and to him, it was all in a day's work.

Out of the miscellaneous menial jobs that the art workers did, and some of the tasks that got left behind by everyone, George made himself a job. He made cedeepee look like a great idea.

Sometimes in the afternoons, George would take a break and come into my office for a chat. He had grown up at an outstation where a Balanda teacher had lived for many years.

'That Jonathan,' he told me, 'He taught me English, writing, everything.' We talked about drinking: 'We're not like you Balanda,' he said, 'You drink a little bit every day, but we Aboriginal people don't do that. We like to drink it all at once and get full way drunk. We're different.'

I looked at him and thought about binge drinking, and disapproval buzzed around in my mind. But then, plenty of Balandas binged on booze too; among the temperate white people in Maningrida this was easy to forget. He's right, I thought, they have their way and we have ours.

These chats were one of the highlights at work. So much of my interaction with Aboriginal people at the art centre was about me wanting to interview them, or them wanting money or favours. But George and I were just talking for the sake of it.

❧ ❧

My flat was at one end of the museum building. The museum was called Djómi, named after a sacred spring in the town, and subtitled 'Maningrida's cultural keeping place'. The Djómi spring was being restored: years of rubbish had accumulated in the water, and now a team was working to clean it up and revegetate some parts of it. What must the water spirit who is said to live there have thought of this? The restoration was headed by Balandas, and the cedeepee workers sometimes went to work and sometimes didn't. When they finished, they were planning to put up a sign to remind people of the significance of the site in the hope that it wouldn't fill up with rubbish again. It was a very Balanda thing to do, I thought—a sign. For Aboriginal people, knowing that it was a water spirit's spring, a fertility site, ought to have been sign enough.

The museum struck me as a very Balanda thing as well. Inside the building was a list of people who had helped make it happen, and the list contained many Aboriginal names. But I knew that a Balanda had had the idea, and got the funding, and come up with the design, and got other Balandas involved with their dehumidifiers and glass cases and white cotton gloves. The Aboriginal people in Maningrida didn't keep much: traditionally, most of their food and their material possessions were organic, so when they were finished, or worn out, or not needed, they could be left to rot or fossilise. This habit of leaving stuff behind and moving on was at the heart of the rubbish problem in the Djómi spring—the habit hadn't changed as rubbish had changed from organic to plastic. And it was also an indication that a museum was not a particularly Aboriginal way of remembering.

A culture known for its stunning oral tradition, which teaches its children to remember stories, facts, names, terrain, surely couldn't have much use or regard for glass cases and text panels.

Despite this, Aboriginal people liked it. Kids used it for school projects, and occasionally adults showed it to visiting Balandas. For a small community museum, the Djómi was impressive. It was mostly used by friends and relations of Balandas living in Maningrida, or by visiting experts, researchers and dignitaries. It housed a collection of art and artefacts that had been put aside by Balandas over the years, accompanied by texts about their origin and use.

I had started to think of the museum as a Balanda artefact in itself. Maybe it was assimilating Aboriginal people to our ideas about preservation, recording and history more than it was supporting and maintaining Aboriginal cultures. It was my job to sweep the museum—huge amounts of dust blew in whenever someone walked in—and as I swept I pondered this. In a culture where houses are a new thing, and where life is still lived mainly outside, a culture with a remarkably practical and utilitarian approach to things, did this museum seem like an uncanny fetish, yet another crazy idea of Balandas, who were well known in Maningrida to be strangely hung up on material goods? Is an Aboriginal basket, with naphthalene flakes inside it, sitting in a glass case in an air-conditioned room, with a small tag next to it that says 'Basket made by Kuninjku artist from *Pandanus spiralis*' an artefact of Kuninjku culture or of ours? I swept under

the case full of ceremonial regalia, I swept under the two huge
conical fish traps of a kind no longer made, I dusted the stand
holding the dugout canoe constructed specially for the museum
several years after the last canoe was made for use, I checked for
mould on the bark paintings and examined the dehumidifiers to
make sure they were working, and I had plenty to think about
as I worked.

One Saturday when Mal came to the museum to look
through some archives, he stopped by for a chat, and I started
talking about the point of the museum. Mosquitoes buzzed.
Outside a Balanda house somewhere a lawnmower whined.

I said, 'It's not really "Aboriginal", is it, if Balandas had the
idea and Balandas have to look after it?'

'But lots of Aboriginal people worked on the project,' Mal
answered. 'And it was all done with the community.'

'Yeah, but it was a Balanda idea in the first place. How do
we know that it's something Aboriginal people want, not just
something *we* think is a good idea?'

'But it's the same with museums everywhere,' said Mal. 'Just
because not everyone in Victoria works at the museum doesn't
mean they don't think it's a good idea to have it.'

I kept going, trying to articulate what had been brewing in
the back of my mind. What would happen if the Balandas stopped
looking after it? Would the community take it on? Mal's responses
were benign and disengaged.

'Well, it's part of the culture office so I'm sure it would be OK,' he said.

We parted cheerily, but the conversation left me dissatisfied. I worried that I hadn't explained my ideas clearly enough, but I knew that Mal was probably not interested in my hypothetical questions anyway.

∽ ∾

My flat had two banks of louvre windows. One of them opened onto trees, with the road beyond them, and the other opened onto the verandah, which was three-quarters closed in with plastic army camouflage netting. A creeper had grown through the netting, forming a solid wall of thick, dried-out canes and thinner, growing tendrils, all of it choked with spiderwebs and dust. It kept the flat dark, and secluded the verandah, making it an ideal place at night for lovers with nowhere else to go. I never heard them, but sometimes in the morning I would find a used black condom in among the pushed-aside chairs.

I decided to take down the wall of netting and replace it with bamboo blinds. Once the blinds had been delivered on the barge, I waited for a dry weekend so that I could spend the day working outside without worrying about humbug. In Melbourne I would have done a project like this with a friend, but this was Maningrida, and I worked alone.

I hacked at the creeper, yanking it out from the netting. I was soon covered in a layer of dust, cobwebs and fine hairs off the creeper stems, all glued together by a coating of sweat, sunscreen and insect repellent. I had to scrunch my eyes closed as I dislodged the woody stems from the ceiling to keep the showers of dust out of them.

Kids were laughing somewhere in the distance as I worked, probably playing in the river. There was a crew of roofers in town, sent by BHP to replace some faulty corrugated iron, and I could hear their nail gun and drilling all day. From time to time a car drove by, or a family walked past on their way through town. As always, I battled a sense of vulnerability. I knew that people probably thought that it was strange for me to be by myself: strange that I didn't have a husband and children; stranger still that I lived without family. Aboriginal people lived and moved in groups, grown ups and kids mingled in, stacked into a car or trailing along through the town. If a small Balanda family unit looked odd, a solo Balanda would seem freakish. Thelma had once asked me whether I had a husband in Melbourne. When I said no, and explained that this wasn't so strange for a twenty-five-year old Balanda, she became acutely embarrassed. It turned out she'd thought I was older than her, perhaps in my early forties. To her, my singleness was so strange that even talking about it seemed extremely rude. Evidently her curiosity had overcome her for a moment, but she soon began to apologise profusely for asking about something that didn't seem embarrassing to me at all.

I worked all day, filthy and sweaty. Finally, I hung the new blinds and swept and rearranged the furniture. From inside, I could now see trees instead of the dark verandah. The light and the sense of accomplishment exalted me. I took a photograph of myself in front of the verandah at the end of the day, my face overexposed by the brightness of the late-afternoon sun, and my smile genuine and bright.

∽ ∾

Nellie came into my office on Wednesday afternoon. She was a weaver, making dilly bags and mats in shades of orange and brown and blue. She had been bringing in a batch of baskets every few weeks, and each time she would come into my office and sit down, and we would have the same conversation. Nellie didn't speak much English, and her few English words were obscured by her thick accent and the fact that several of her teeth were missing. She had to repeat herself a few times before I figured out what she was saying. As usual, we said hello, and then she leant forward and said, 'Ton . . . Gan-burr-ah . . . bipty dollar . . . you-ring-im-up.' She left a long pause between each word, as though she was talking to a simpleton.

When Don, the visiting anthropologist from Canberra, had last been here, he asked Nellie to make him a dilly bag—the special kind used for ceremonies. He gave her $50, and told her to bring the basket to me when it was finished for a second payment of $50. She duly came in, I gave her the $50, she gave me the basket and I thought that that would be it. But we had been having this conversation over and over again ever since.

I was sorting through photographs for the weaving book when Nellie came in, so I showed them to her. She went through the stack of polaroids methodically, without showing any interest in them, until she came to a photo of one of her own baskets. That photo she picked out of the pile and, giving a huge smile, she brought it to her lips and kissed it, saying, 'Nellie, that one, Nellie mag-im.' There was lots of smiling and nodding, with me saying that her baskets were very beautiful. When she had gone, I decided to ask Thelma for help: without an interpreter the issue of payment for Don's basket would never be resolved.

Because Thelma spoke fluent English and was literate and intelligent, she was always in demand with Balandas. I tried not to ask her to do anything, because I knew that she juggled family commitments, work at the JET centre and her interpreting course, along with a constant stream of other requests. Visiting Balandas would ask Thelma to be involved in a whole range of projects— she was easy to work with, because she could meet us halfway across the cultural divide.

I found Thelma at the JET centre, and explained the situation. She agreed to talk to Nellie about it. A few days later, I saw Thelma in the Bawinanga office, and she told me that she had seen Nellie up in Top Camp and asked her about the money. Nellie hadn't realised that the $50 I had given her was from

Don. Thelma explained that she now had the agreed $100 from Don, and the confusion was gone.

⚭ ⚭

The phone was ringing. My mind struggled to work out what was going on, what day it was . . . when I heard Alice's voice. I had slept through my alarm—again. The Build Up was true to its name, the weather getting more humid every week. I had overslept a few times, having lain awake half the night in my windowless, airless bedroom. I would come home from work and feel the floor tiles warm under my feet. Cups, plates and cutlery came warm out of the cupboards. Dry biscuits and chips went limp in the damp air. We were all oppressed by the heat.

I went to work in the daze that comes from being jolted out of a deep sleep. I pushed my mind to wake up and engage with the work I had to do. I knew I had to get the language project started, but I had found working on it even more difficult since the conference in Alice Springs. My faith in language work had given way to doubts about the value of yet another project initiated by Balandas on behalf of the Aboriginal community.

The Balandas were committed to the project of writing everything down and recording for the future. Meanwhile, Aboriginal languages and cultures thrived on the outstations. One of my favourite things about living in Maningrida was being able to see nine different groups speaking different languages, performing different ceremonies and producing different kinds of art. The languages of some of the smaller groups were giving way to the languages of bigger groups, but English was barely making an impact. Children didn't speak English until they went to school.

But my colleagues and I believed that a dictionary project was an inherently good thing. We thought that, even if the people we knew had no need for a dictionary of their language, their descendants might. We wanted everything written down so that it could be saved.

Alice and I had planned the structure of the project. A different linguist would work on each language, and train a speaker as a language worker. We hoped that Maningrida would get a language centre one day—the Balanda linguists who had worked on the region's languages were all supportive of this idea—and so one of the aims of the project was to train local people who might be interested in working with a future language centre. The linguists were responsible for producing a dictionary and a guide written in simple English. Using English, which most Aboriginal people in the region didn't speak particularly well, and used only to speak to Balandas, showed that we assumed that these books would be useful when the local languages had declined and English had taken hold.

All of these doubts went around in my head as I opened the file and tried to figure out where to start. It wasn't that I thought it was a 'bad' project. The linguists involved had good relationships with the people they worked with, and the speakers were happy to work on the projects. But I struggled with it because it wasn't Aboriginal self-determination.

It seemed that the job of Balandas in Maningrida was to protect Aboriginal people from filling in forms and the onerous responsibilities that engaging with bureaucracy brings. So we had designed the language project, and written its twenty-page application for funding. We had come up with its million-dollar budget, and then revised the budget down to the amount of funding we were given. As I grappled with application forms, budget requirements and requesting 'variations', struggling to learn the language of government funding, I could only imagine how much more difficult it would be for someone who spoke English as a second (or third, or fourth) language and had only rudimentary secondary education. The Balandas all meant well by trying to protect Aboriginal people from all of this, but I had begun to wonder whether we were also protecting them from the flip side of this onerous bureaucracy—real understanding of, and engagement with, systems of power.

There was no place for this thinking in my work. The art centre had a grant from ATSIC, and it was my job to spend the money and produce results. I began the project by contacting the linguists who had worked on the languages, and asking them how they would like to begin. It would be easy enough to run the language project, I told myself, as long as I tucked my doubts away and broke it down into a series of small tasks that in themselves were surely benign.

∽ ∾

The artists switched from bark painting to carving as the sap dried out of the trees. Through the Dry Season the bark clung to the trunk and couldn't be prised off to be used as a canvas. Instead, a soft-wood tree was harvested and each trunk became a spirit figure—a mimih, a skinny, cheeky spirit who lived in the rock country; or a yawkyawk, a water spirit a bit like a mermaid; or a buluwana, who had no arms. Artists tended to make the spirits in their own likeness—so the thin men brought in thin figures, and the short, fatter men brought in plumper sculptures.

George came to work one morning with two stout figures. When I walked through the warehouse later, I noticed that he wasn't there.

'He stormed off in a huff this morning,' Alice explained. 'He reckons I didn't pay him enough for his sculptures. Look at them—I gave him more than they were worth, but he was outraged.'

George's art was of the same mid-range quality as most of the art we bought. Only about ten or twenty per cent of work would end up in fine art exhibitions, and at the other end of the spectrum, only a very small percentage was so bad that it wouldn't sell. Most of it was average, some finer and particularly well done, some rougher and less well painted, but still within the same range.

During the afternoon, I heard a man yelling and went to see what was going on. George had come back to pick up his dispute with Alice. He was tense and red with rage, and his voice was husky.

'You pay Jimmy $500, and you only pay me $100!' he was saying. 'You have to give me more money!'

Alice tried to explain that Jimmy was the centre's most famous artist, and galleries would pay a lot for his work. Everybody else was paid about the same.

'Look, these mimihs from Tommy,' she said, 'I paid him $100, same as you. And this buluwana from Joshua, $100.'

But George didn't seem to hear. His anger seemed to intensify before our eyes. He was barely able to speak, resorting to swearing at Alice with the full force of his rage. He suddenly looked mean and frightening.

'You bitch! If you don't give me two hundred, I come back and get you bitch with a spear.'

Alice said calmly, 'I can't give you any more money.'

He stormed out, punching the roller door as he went. We were left with a shocked silence.

'Are you OK?' I asked.

'Yeah, I'm fine.'

'Do you think he'll come back?'

'I don't know. It's happened before with other artists.'

Ron suggested that Alice keep the art centre locked for the day, just in case. We all went back to our offices. It felt as though

George had been possessed by a different person. I thought about the reason for his outburst. He worked with the paintings and sculptures every day, moving them, treating them for mould and borer, packing them and shipping them. Each work had a tag attached to it with the artist's name on it, and a price. He would have seen again and again that some paintings were sold for $80 and others for $3,000, and he would have seen that although the size of the work was part of its cost, there were other factors involved as well. And yet he seemed to know as little as anyone about the pricing system.

He might have been frustrated that, although he had carved a job for himself out of various menial tasks and although he had made friends with everyone, the real power in the centre was in the hands of the Balandas. Balandas worked with computers and phones in English, in air conditioned offices, and he worked with cardboard and a broom in a hot, sweaty warehouse.

He might have been enraged by the subtle ways that the art centre and the town were white-run and, unable to put his rage into words, distilled it instead into a demand for more money— the ultimate elusive Balanda commodity.

His rage was crudely articulated as his English failed him. George was one of the people who breathed life into the hope that Aboriginal people could take on more of the white world without having to forgo their own language and culture.

Now he was gone.

The warehouse was hotter than ever: it was the annual fraying of tempers. November ticked towards December. The Balandas were all hoping for rain, and waiting to fly south for Christmas.

∽ ∾

I drove out to Rocky Point with Ron and Sue, an hour from town in their four-wheel drive over rutted dirt roads. It was worth the drive, as it always was: the stunning tropical beach seemed to go for miles, laid bare by the ebbing tide. Ron and Sue had been fishing there a few weeks ago, and had to race the tide back to the car when it turned and ran in towards the shore. The best fishing was on the changing tides, but the water moved fast— and there were crocodiles in the creek as well as the sea.

But there was no running that day. We went for a long walk, relaxed around each other. It was good to be out of town, breathing in the salt and talking about parts of our lives that were bigger than Maningrida. We were swapping histories, the way that new friends do. I kept thinking of how different we were but it didn't matter—we were slowly building a friendship together.

And then the light was ebbing with the tide, and we were heading back to the car. The air was thick and damp, as it was all the time by then. But just as we reached the truck, the weather broke, and my first tropical raindrops splashed onto my skin. We drove home through rain, and watching the drops hit the car windows made me feel at home. There was a sense of physical relief as at last, some of the moisture fell out of the air. The ground was so dried out that the water ran over the top of it instead of soaking in. But the smell of rain was different to the smell of humidity, and for the first time in months, the air moved in a cool breeze.

Six

THE RAIN REFUSED TO FALL AGAIN. THE WEATHER WAS SO HOT AND humid that I could feel my body going blurry at its edges. In Melbourne, my skin had been clearly defined, but in the relentless heat it seemed to melt slightly, as an unlit candle does.

I had been perching uncomfortably at Simon's spindly tin table for months, crouching on the small chairs, trying to find a comfortable way of arranging my legs around the table's legs. When I tried to write, my elbow fell off the table; I ate by balancing my plate and water glass on its tiny surface. It rocked, because it was so flimsy, and I worried about my laptop falling off and crashing onto the hard tile floor. I had ordered a new wooden table and six chairs from Darwin.

They arrived on Thursday's barge, and Sue came over that night to help me put the table together, bringing along a contraband bottle of vodka. As she made us vodka and tonics, she told me about her arrival in Maningrida: she had dropped her bag as she got off the plane, and the gin she was smuggling in spilt all over the tarmac. She panicked, all too aware that bringing spirits in was illegal, but everyone just ignored what had happened and carried on with unloading the bags. Everybody turned a blind eye to Balanda alcohol consumption.

When we had put the table together, we made some dinner and then sat down to eat, luxuriating in the expanse of tabletop under our arms.

There was to be no more perching. I was making the flat my own. I was stretching out into my job. And I was discovering the size and shape of my place in the community. When Sue had gone home, I stood with my palms pressed flat on the tabletop for a long time, feeling the solidity of wood supported by four strong legs.

∽ ∾

The next morning, Alice and I were talking about documentations for paintings by a new artist called Billy Wilson. His relatives had brought them in from his outstation. They were paintings of average quality, mainly of fish, similar to many of the secular paintings done by mid-range artists. They were most likely to sell to the tourist market, unless a gallery owner took a particular liking to them and elevated them to the category 'art'.

Carol came over from the school. She had been in Maningrida ten years and seemed to know everyone, so Alice asked her whether she knew anything about Billy.

'The only thing to do with anything he sends you,' she said 'is take a match to it.' Seeing our shocked faces, Carol went on: 'I'm sorry, girls, but that bastard murdered his wife, Nancy, and she was such a lovely lovely woman.' She explained that Nancy, who had worked at the school with her, was regularly beaten up by Billy and would come to her house sometimes to escape further beatings. Eventually, Billy killed her, and went to prison. And now he was back home—and making art work.

I was upset by this story, and I could see that Alice was just as disturbed. I had heard things like this before. Every so often someone would be prompted to tell an old, terrible story like this. I knew that women were bashed, raped and assaulted every time grog came into town—an outbreak of violence at least once a fortnight. I'd been told that it was common for men to bash their wives when the women returned from a holiday or trip *just in case* they had done anything wrong while they were away. It was out there, in the houses all around me.

I thought of Kenny, who had been jailed for sexually assaulting his daughter. I would often see him in the Bawinanga office, and he was always friendly, and I couldn't think of a better option than being friendly in return. Later, I would think about our interaction, wondering whether my friendliness was somehow hypocritical. Would it be more principled, somehow, to scorn his greetings and chat? Would that do any good for the Aboriginal women he lived alongside? Unlike me, they were not just passing through.

Carol went on to tell us about another man, who had set fire to his wife. I felt my insides go cold and rigid, and I felt the hot swell of tears behind my eyes. When she got up to leave, I thought how much worse this must feel for her, with her memories of the women we'd talked about, their lives and their funerals and their senseless deaths.

There was nothing to do but go back to work.

⤴ ⤴

A week later, on the first Sunday morning of December, I was at home waiting for Ron to come by and collect me for a day's fishing. I was keeping an ear out for his car, an ancient four-wheel-drive landcruiser pulling a boat trailer. There was a knock on my door—strange—in Maningrida most people called out rather than coming up to a house.

I opened the door wide to find a young Aboriginal man who I didn't know standing there. He looked like any of the young men around town, a bit taller than me, slim, his curly hair cut short. He was dressed typically in a bright yellow basketball singlet and dark floppy shorts, and his feet were bare.

He asked, 'Is Simon there?'

I gave him my usual answer to this question: 'He's with his family, in Sydney.'

Instead of leaving, this man stayed, casting around for other things to ask me. Now I noticed that he wasn't entirely typical: he had an edgy, nervous manner, his eyes darting around and his body moving constantly from foot to foot. He kept one hand behind his back while we talked, and held on tight to his elbow with his other hand.

'I want to look at photographs,' he said. 'Simon got photographs. Can I look?'

I told him I didn't have any photographs.

His approach became more direct: 'Can I come inside?' He was softly spoken, wheedling his requests.

'What's your name?' I asked.

'Rodney—I mean, Roger,' he said in a fumbling fashion.

He was bigger than me, and stronger, and he had stepped forward so that he was standing just inside my living room, only centimetres away from me. I tried to think of a way to get rid of him without aggravating him. Like all Balandas, I was used to being humbugged by Aboriginal people wanting money or a lift to their country. I had learnt that it was better to make an excuse than to give a blank refusal, which could be offensive.

Eventually, I suggested that he could go into the museum and look at the photos in there. I opened the museum up, turned on the lights and then closed the door behind me. A minute later he was back. I told myself that he was probably just stoned and bored. But there was something strange in his manner, and now I was really anxious.

He asked to come in again. I opened the door, but this time I blocked his way, the doorhandle smooth in my sweating hand, the tiles slightly rough under my bare feet. Again and again I said,

'I'm too busy, I'm sorry.' It wasn't working. I would have to think of a better way of persuading him to leave.

Then he leant in towards me, and with his face very close to mine said, 'Will you have sex with me?'

Terror bolted through me. 'Go away!' I said, in the strongest voice I could find.

He retreated slightly but stood there, whining, 'You gotta help me.'

My doorway was hidden from the street, and I had no close neighbours. If he tried anything, there would be no-one around to help me or even to hear that something was going on. He kept asking me to have sex with him. I kept saying no. Then, desperate, I suggested that he go back to the museum, hoping that I might be able to persuade him to leave without making him angry. I could feel my heart pumping and my hands shaking as I held on to the door.

Suddenly he reached out and groped my crotch. I reacted without thinking, pushed him out the door, slammed it and locked it. He kept calling out to me from the verandah—'Excuse me, excuse me.'

I phoned Ron and Sue, struggling to push the right numbers on the phone through my panic. I could barely speak, but I finally explained and Ron arrived in about a minute. I cowered in my flat and listened to their conversation. I heard Ron say, 'Are you hassling this woman?' but couldn't make out the reply.

Ron told me that he had said he was just looking for Simon, and then he left.

∽ ∾

I went to Ron and Sue's and then we went out fishing as usual. We talked a bit about what had happened and my friends reassured me. For most of the day I forgot about it, concentrating on the fishing or the conversation, glad to be distracted. From time to time I would remember, feeling the memory through my whole body. But it seemed best to act normal and unafraid. What would be the use of falling apart?

The water was calm, glassy, grey, reflecting the colours of the Build Up clouds that filled the sky. There was no storm, no rain, just the heat and the humidity, relieved at last by the boat moving fast through the salty air and the splash of cold sea water on our skin.

I always felt a kind of sadness as we sped back into town after these Sundays out on the boat. The sun was setting and there was a kind of melancholy about returning from the freedom of the boat's movement on the water to the quietness and stillness of the town. Today, this customary sadness was undercut by fear. I had to go back to my flat and face what had happened there. How would I be able to sleep?

Ron walked me to my front door to make sure no-one was there. It was all clear, and I stepped inside. My bright 'social' face dissolved as I washed a day of salt and sweat and sunscreen off my skin. I burst into tears and let the fear fall down my face.

An hour later, I was feeling much calmer, thinking about making dinner, when I heard a voice on the verandah calling out to me: *'Excuse me, excuse me'*—the voice from this morning. My body and mind were instantly alive with fear: what was he going to do? I rang Alice in tears, asking her to come and get me. By the time she arrived, Rodney/Roger was gone. I had thrown some clothes in a bag and I was ready to leave.

∽ ∾

The next day, the story spread and people came to offer their support and concern. Archie said that Bawinanga would do whatever I wanted to make the flat safe. He suggested enclosing the verandah in the same heavy wire mesh that covered the Bawinanga windows. I said I would think about it. I didn't want to live in a cage. But I did want to be safe.

Denise, who worked at the school making readers for the bilingual programs, came in to offer her sympathy. She told me that when she first arrived she had woken up one night to find an Aboriginal man standing over her bed. She had gotten rid of him somehow—she didn't explain how.

'I slept with a carving knife under my pillow after that,' she said. 'Until I got married, of course.'

I had been holding on to the fact that Rodney/Roger hadn't made it far beyond my doorway. Denise's story made me feel that the walls of my flat were permeable.

Sue invited me to have dinner at their house that night, saying, 'You don't want to be sitting at home stewing about it, wondering if he's about to turn up.' I was grateful for the company, and even more grateful when they drove me home, even though their house was three minutes' walk away.

It was late, and I went straight to bed, reading until I was tired enough to sleep. On Tuesday, I began to feel better. Monday had been uneventful, and I thought that if I could put the encounter behind me I could start to feel safe again.

I spent the evening alone in my flat, determined to assume that everything would be fine. And then I heard the now-familiar voice calling out to me from my verandah: '*Excuse me, excuse me.*' Once again a panic-stricken phone call. Once again I fled to Alice and Mal's house. This time we decided that I wasn't going back.

Between my experience and the stories I was being told, I had started to feel like there was no escape from violence in Maningrida. It seemed that this kind of thing was normal. Every young Aboriginal man I saw made me feel afraid. I was ashamed of this feeling, thinking that I was being racist. But the thin men of eighteen or nineteen wearing floppy oversized shorts and basketball singlets were similar enough to Rodney to be a jolting reminder of what had happened.

❧ ❧

The following Friday, Archie and his wife, Patsy, came to Alice and Mal's for dinner. Somehow a story came up about a man who had kept his family under the constant threat of violence at the point of a gun. I stared at my plate: for me, this felt like one violent story too many. I didn't think that I could keep sitting through conversations that went like this.

As the main course came to an end, the phone rang. It was my older sister. She had called the flat and heard the message giving Alice and Mal's phone number.

'Our father's dead,' she said.

I hadn't seen our father for years, and hadn't thought about him for months. I was as confused to be talking about him at all as to be hearing of his death.

'What?' I said. 'How weird.'

'He was in a car crash at the train crossing.'

'What crossing?' I asked.

'You know, there was a railway crossing near his house . . .'

I did vaguely remember this from childhood access visits. She went on to explain that the accident might have been caused by his Parkinson's disease—something I hadn't even known he suffered from.

When I told my sisters I was coming here, they asked me if I would be safe. My brothers and sisters and I knew all about fear: we were raised on it. We knew, from our insides out, that if you couldn't be sure that you were safe it was like freefalling in nothingness. As we talked about our father, I thought of the guns he kept in his wardrobe, the memory making me feel cold and tight with fear.

On hearing the news of his death, my sister told me, one of our other sisters had said to another, 'Maybe now we can stop having nightmares.'

I put the phone down and walked quietly past the dinner table and out the door. Once I was outside, I began to cry. The tears were not for the loss of a man I barely knew, but for the pain of a childhood spent in fear of his violence, for the scars he had left on me and my brothers and sisters, for the sadness and grief that had come with the absence of a loving father and the presence instead of this terrifying man.

∽ ∾

I was four and a half when my parents separated, and every conversation I heard about violence in the community brought back the memory I had of those early years. In Maningrida, the stories were told from a safe place on the 'us' side of the 'us and them' divide. The people who told them spoke as though violence and terror belonged only to Aboriginal families and it was our role to sympathise and to exclaim in dismay. If only I could have shared their distance.

I had tried not to burden anyone with the terrible truth: the fact that I was glad that my father was dead, that I felt his death made the world safer. This was too shocking for most people to understand.

And yet, in Maningrida, violence, abuse, threats, terror, were all just a part of life. For example, when a white woman was raped by an Aboriginal man some years before, a contingent of white women went to the council asking that something be done. The Aboriginal women on the council told them that nothing could be done—and they would have known. They lived with this kind of thing every day. Indeed, Valerie, who had given me my skin name, had come into the art centre one Monday after a barge weekend with a bruised face. She asked Alice for money so that she could get out of Maningrida and away from her husband. Alice had given her an advance on future artwork of a few hundred dollars, but had told me later that she had seen Valerie go through this many times before—deciding she would leave but never actually going away.

The next day, Ron and Sue left for their Christmas holiday and I moved into their house. They lived in half of a duplex, with Jenny, Bawinanga's bookkeeper, in the other half. Daisy, one of the Bawinanga workers, and her family lived next door, in a house always full of people and activity, trucks coming and going from outstations, and kids playing on the verandah. Before she left, Sue said, 'I told Daisy what happened, so she'll keep an eye on you.' And she did: not long after I arrived she called out to me to say hello. Because she was quiet, I had assumed that she didn't speak much English. But I realised I was wrong as she told me to let her know if I needed anything.

As well as being surrounded by people, I was living with the rivermouth twenty metres away. The water was a calming and beautiful presence, somehow reassuring. I made a cup of tea and sat on the verandah looking at the river. Once again I had my own space, but this time, I felt safe in it. All I had to do now was survive until five o'clock next Friday when the plane would take me away.

Seven

I SAT IN MY FAVOURITE MELBOURNE CAFÉ, WAITING FOR MY FRIEND Shelley. I was buzzing on half a glass of coffee—six months of home-made coffee had reduced my tolerance for strong espresso. I had spent so much time over the years sitting in cafés like this, drinking coffee like this, watching street scenes like this. Eighteen months before, I had come here a lot. I was writing my honours thesis and I would bribe myself to do the most difficult work with French toast and coffee. Today, like those distant mornings, I was surrounded by people reading the paper, having meetings, spending time with friends. I took comfort from them, from the crowds outside, from the shop signs and trams and the sounds of the city, from the sheer numbers of people surrounding me. There was a deep familiarity in this experience, a sense of belonging.

I was thinking about not returning to Maningrida. I could send for my things, I thought, and just stay here. My holiday had made me feel stronger and safer, but I had a growing fear that this sense of security came from my friends and family and Melbourne itself, rather than from me. Would going back to Maningrida mean a return to powerlessness and danger?

Shelley arrived, and we talked about my concerns. 'Are you afraid he'll come back?' she asked.

'Yeah, I suppose so. But also—now I feel like there's so much violence in the town, and what happened to me was actually pretty mild . . . is that really the kind of place I want to live?'

'No-one wants you to go back if you're not going to be safe,' she said. 'We want you here!'

'The thing is,' I admitted, 'I'm not ready to leave Maningrida. I worked so hard at fitting in, making friends, getting used to living there . . . I feel like just as I was getting good at it, this happened.'

Shelley reassured me that no-one would think I was a failure if I left.

Eventually I said, 'It's not that. If I don't go back, it will feel like he won somehow, or he pushed me out—it would always be unfinished.'

She asked me what would make me feel better about going back. I thought for a long time before saying, 'Knowing I could leave if I wanted to.'

So I made a deal with myself: I would go back and see what it was like, and if I didn't like it or I didn't feel safe, I would leave. There was a wedding in Melbourne in March: if I needed to, I could buy a one-way ticket home then. I was giving Maningrida a six-week second chance.

∽ ∾

I arrived back on a Sunday afternoon. Once again the plane tilted towards the town as it descended. Once again the rivermouth gleamed blue in the foreground, and a minute later the tin-shed airport appeared with a cluster of trucks behind it. But this time it was all familiar to me: I could see my flat, and the art centre, and Alice's truck driving along the road towards the airport to pick me up.

My flat was smaller than I remembered it, and bigger at the same time—the familiar-unfamiliar feeling that comes with time away. Alice had been in to open the windows and turn the fans on, and she had put a vase of flowers on my new table to welcome me. My eyes took in my teapot in its place on the bench, my photos on the fridge, and my books on the shelf. I had almost forgotten that this was my home, so I had not expected the feeling of relief that a homecoming can bring.

I put on a new CD and unpacked, then put up the new curtains I had brought back with me: blue and green, thick enough to prevent people looking in, but light enough so that air could still come into the flat. I was conscious of my new security door, a layer of protection between me and whoever or whatever might be on my verandah. Finally, I put on some washing and made a pot of tea. It had taken an afternoon to resettle.

I was prepared to leave Maningrida if I had to. But I was determined to stay.

෪ ෨

Walking into the art centre after three weeks away was walking into air thick with the smell of pandanus and reeds and bark. The smell of the bush, imperceptible when breathed every day, now struck me afresh. I also noticed that the centre was full: there were baskets, paintings, bags and mats everywhere.

'Belinj!' Alice greeted me with the Kuninjku skin name Valerie had given me. 'Welcome back!'

'Godjok,' I replied, 'Good to see you!'

'How are you going? Gamak?'

'Yo, gamak.'

I hadn't spoken this Balanda language for three weeks: English scattered with phrases and words from Aboriginal English and from Aboriginal languages. I was back in Maningrida, back at work—back to being a Balanda.

Alice introduced me to the new workers. Most people moved into town from their outstations in the Wet to avoid being stranded when the rivers rose, but these young men had come in to play footy.

'Guys, this is Mary Ellen, she works in the culture office. Mary Ellen, this is Samson, this is Ricky, Norris and Horace.'

They were all from Yilan, about a hundred kilometres away on the coast, a place I imagined as full of two-dimensional fish and shellfish because that was what I had seen in the many paintings of it I had documented.

I felt a bit shy around this strong, cohesive, Burrara-speaking group, so for the first day or two we just smiled at each other. Gradually I got to know them, and to remember which brother was Horace and which was Norris. Samson was very friendly, and a bit of a show-off. In repose, his face was serious, intelligent, almost frowning. But he was always moving—dance steps, or exaggerated facial expressions and gestures. Ricky was smaller, thinner and quieter. He seemed to be laughing all the time— mostly at Samson's jokes—and he put a lot of effort into his hair. It would be bright yellow one week, half shaved off the next. Norris and Horace were both big, soft men. Norris had a serious, unhurried demeanour, and I couldn't tell how much of our English conversations he understood. I realised that I had met Horace before when he had come to work for a day or two a few months ago. He had been contemptuous when I'd asked him to stop smoking in the storeroom full of the most valuable art, and had 'delegated' everything he'd been asked to do to one of the other guys. His manner had been cavalier and impatient, but now he seemed to be part of the team.

We soon realised that the group revolved around Samson. He was more of an exhibitionist and an attention-seeker than any of the other Aboriginal people I met, the first to switch to English when a Balanda walked by, to make a joke, to flirt or just to say hello or make conversation. He took to wearing a spangly dangly diamante earring in one ear, and was always dancing around the offices, traditional dances interspersed with hip-hop moves.

The atmosphere in the centre changed with its cedeepee workers. George's hard-working but friendly demeanour had taken over the whole warehouse. The Yilan boys brought in a young, playful, energetic vibe. They would joke and dance and listen to rap music, and there was a constant flow of Burarra and laughter in the air. Girls who probably should have been at school would stop by to chat and flirt; boys would come in to cadge cigarettes. In the mornings, someone was always on their way to the Hasty Tasty take-away, or the school canteen.

The Wet Season brought mould. It crept over furniture, walls, books, anything. People would come back from a holiday to find a green patina over the inside of their house. At the art centre it was like a monster that had to be constantly placated— and this was the job of the Yilan boys. They would put on large, black gas masks, brush the mould off the paintings, and then spray them with Glen 20 in an attempt to prevent it from returning. At the same time, they were battling insects. The borer that always threatened the sculptures and bark paintings were even worse at this time of year, so there was an endless regime of freezing artworks to kill the parasites, and cleaning up the little piles of dust left behind in the wake of the little holes the borer made. On top of that, there was the usual cleaning and packing work. We had become a bustling workplace, where all the cedeepee workers had enough to do.

∽ ∾

I sat with Sue and Ron on their verandah watching the sunset. The sky was lit briefly with orange, but Wet Season sunsets were never as spectacular as the picture-postcard orange and pink skies that appeared every night in the Dry. My friends had spent Christmas trekking in Nepal, and they were explaining the differences between the third-world conditions there and in Maningrida.

Sue said, 'We think things are bad here, but going over there really put things in perspective.'

In Nepal they had seen families working long hours in menial or back-breaking labouring jobs to scrape together the money for their children's education. There was no welfare system over there, so everyone had to work. They were constantly struggling to make things better for their families.

Ron drew the contrast with Maningrida, where education was provided for free but hardly anyone sent their children to school, and where people were generally reliant on welfare rather than work for a cash income.

'I'm not convinced we're helping any more,' he added. 'Actually, I think we're part of the problem more than anything else. As long as there are all these Balandas doing all the jobs, there's no incentive for Aborigines to send their children to school so that they can take over.'

Sue said she had become disillusioned about her job. 'I provide all this Balanda education, but it doesn't change anything,' she said. 'Who do we think we're kidding? Let's face it, the Aborigines are not going to take on our jobs and make us redundant.'

'The thing is,' Ron said, 'our jobs are getting more complicated all the time, so we rely more on computers and databases and things, which just makes it even harder for an Aborigine to be able to do the work.'

'That's definitely what's happening at the art centre,' I admitted. 'We've just got a grant to buy some new computers, and we've been working on the website—it's hardly "Aboriginalisation".'

It was the first conversation I'd had in Maningrida that was critical of the role of Balandas. Although we talked about Maningrida all the time, most Balandas either said it was a privilege to work there, or they implied that they were powerless and that the problems rested with the Aboriginal community. More often than not, we would talk about the problems without really analysing their causes or possible solutions. It was a relief to hear my friends saying some of the things I had been thinking to myself for the last few months.

'This is why we usually avoid talking about "Maningrida",' Sue said, with heavy emphasis on the last word. 'It gets so depressing.'

When it was time for me to leave, Ron drove me home. This had become our new routine: since December I had decided never to walk anywhere after dark by myself. He waited in the car while I opened my security door and the front door. I turned on the lights, and locked both doors behind me. Things were getting back to normal—my flat had become my own again.

∽ ∾

I had heard a lot about Phil, a full-time staff member, who had left the week I arrived. I had never met him, but I felt his presence still inhabited the art centre. He'd gone to Darwin on a drinking binge and hadn't been seen in Maningrida since. Now he was living out at Yilan with his family. The job of Aboriginal heritage officer had been created for him a couple of years before this. He was supposed to work with the arts office and the culture office on Aboriginal culture, but he had done less and less until finally he had collapsed under the pressure, disappearing without telling anyone that he was going, under a cloud of talk about money that was said to have gone to Darwin when it was meant to go to a funeral ceremony.

Often, when I spoke to people outside the community, Phil's name would come up. If I commented on the difficulty of getting Aboriginal people involved in work, they would recommend that I speak to Phil. If I talked about how the art centre worked, or what we hoped our website might do, or what the culture office was doing, the Balanda I was talking to would respond with a story about Phil and how he could solve whatever the problem was. He was the man who could bridge the two cultures, the man who would Aboriginalise the centre, the man who could be relied on for a Balanda-friendly interpretation of his culture, or for liaison with Aboriginal people.

How was it possible that so many Balandas from Melbourne, Sydney, Canberra or Darwin could speak to me so confidently about him? He was one of the rare Balanda-friendly Aboriginal people who was relied on far too heavily to represent his community. It started to seem unsurprising that he had fallen apart. He had said that he never wanted to run the art centre, because it would be too much humbug, with relatives demanding what he should give them by Burarra law, but could not give them by Balanda law. He must have been under pressure all the time from his family for money, as one of the few Aboriginal people in town with a salary rather than cedeepee and top-up. And every visiting Balanda, along with several of the resident Balandas, had rested their hopes for the community on his shoulders.

In the six months since he left, Alice had used the funding for his salary to employ a few temporary people to help out. Finally, when Beck left and Alice was faced with the task of finding a new admin assistant, she decided to recruit an information technology officer as well. Quietly, unobtrusively, the Aboriginal heritage officer salary clicked over from Burarra to Balanda.

It was difficult to get staff in Maningrida. Carol had once joked that there used to be a saying at the school that any potential teacher needed two attributes: they had to be upright and warm. The process of finding staff began with a job ad in the *Australian* and, if you were lucky, CVs would dribble in from the few people who were willing to live and work in such a remote place. They were interviewed by telephone: flying people in was extremely expensive and so tended to be a last resort.

The jobs went to Jodie and Brad, a twenty-one-year-old couple from Perth. They had the right skills for their jobs, and they seemed keen to live in an Aboriginal community. We knew we were lucky to get them.

Brad was a textbook computer nerd, down to his unnaturally pale skin and remarkably oversized runners. We needed him because there was funding to buy new computers, as well as a digital camera for recording the artworks and for online sales. Brad was to buy all the equipment and set up a network for the machines, as well as finishing off the website Beck had begun. Jodie's job was similar to Beck's: general administrative work, stock control, banking and supervising the cedeepee staff.

Jodie was a flirt. While Alice and I tended to wear boots, cotton pants or skirts and t-shirts—like most of the women in Maningrida, we were practical, no-nonsense types—Jodie was all nonsense—friendly, outgoing, but simpering and girlish at the same time. She came to work in our hot, dusty office in wafty white dresses and strappy sandals, and batted her eyelids at the workers.

I was constantly critical of her. It was all too easy to slide into Balanda complacency—to feel a sense of superiority in how long you had been in the community, and simply in the fact that you lived there at all. This went way beyond Maningrida; people who had lived in Darwin twenty, ten or even five years would sneeringly ask newcomers, 'How long have you been in the Territory?' as though it were an endurance test that they were winning. At its most extreme, it meant that long-term residents refused to tolerate any new ideas. It was an easy way of being an expert, where skills and knowledge were simply equated with years spent north of the Tropic of Capricorn.

But there was a much less extreme, and therefore more insidious, version of the same thing. It was a covert, relentless competition among Balandas where each tried to prove that they were better at talking to Aboriginal people than the others—more ethical, less racist, less patronising, more egalitarian. When I felt the smug tight smile of victory on my face, I realised I had started to play this game with Jodie. I was disgusted with myself for buying into it and made an effort to stop.

ᔥ ᔦ

I walked into the arts office and heard Alice on the phone. 'No, Valerie, I can't send you that money. You got no money. When that print sells, I sendim that money.' After a pause I heard 'OK, Valerie, bobo.'

Alice sighed heavily as she put the phone down. 'That's the second time Valerie's called this week,' she said. 'She's always drunk and I can't get any sense out of her.'

Valerie had been in Darwin since January, and didn't seem to be planning to come home. I missed her coming into the art centre. I had always liked her warmth and her sense of humour; now I was worried about her.

∽ ∾

I went back into my office, where there was an exhibition of paintings—propped on benches and shelves, leaning against cupboards. Whenever I looked up, my eyes caught an expanse of fine cross-hatching, or a goanna, or a tree. I had spoken to the artist, Jack, to get the story for each painting, and now I had to print out the documentation, sign its certification of authenticity and stick it onto the back of the painting.

Jack was a small man in his forties, thin and fine like his brushstrokes, with loose curly hair cropped short. He had deep-set eyes, hollow cheeks and a wide, thin mouth. Either because he was shy, or because his English wasn't good enough to sustain a conversation, he didn't have much to say, although he always seemed friendly. But the documentations were easy, because these paintings were the same as others he had done before. I could just copy out the old stories. All I had needed to do was make sure that the stories were right, rather than interviewing him for new information.

Each male artist was authorised to paint certain topics, usually their Dreaming. They could ask permission of certain relatives to paint some topics, but others were entirely forbidden to them. Anyone could paint secular things, like fish or plants. Men would sometimes authorise a wife or daughter to paint their Dreaming, but in general, men painted and women worked with fibre. Because of these rules, there was a limited set of themes to paint. The best artists varied the composition and interpretation of these themes, coming up with stunning new interpretations. Others, like Jack, tended to paint the same story the same way each time. But Jack's brushstrokes were so delicate, and his paintings so beautifully executed, that he was considered to be a fine artist. These paintings were for a solo show in Sydney. Only the best artists could sustain a show in their own right, rather than having their work incorporated into group shows.

The painting my eyes fell on most often was covered in cross-hatching, stretching in a strong diagonal from top left to bottom right in the top half, and then turning back the other way in the bottom half, with a stripe of cross-hatching in between. It was predominantly white and pale brown. There were two circles in each half of the painting, and within each, the cross-hatching was turned a different way against its background.

'That's my Dreaming,' Jack had said, going on to explain that this design would be painted on his chest for ceremony.

I knew that a Dreaming was related to a person's country, and their identity, ceremonial songs and dances. Jack had told me that he had a relationship with his Dreaming, and had to do good things for it, such as painting it. He also described talking to his Dreaming, saying that when he went to that site on his country, he would ask the Dreaming to keep him safe, and it would—as long as he had looked after it properly. These paintings seemed to be simultaneously an act of commerce and an act of religion.

Commerce was always part of it. When the artists were paid for their art, they often took the money to the shop for food and cigarettes, or to the workshop for repairs on their cars, or they would gamble with it or give it away to friends and family. Some would leave it at the art centre to go into a savings account for a new truck. Many people relied on their art as a weekly, fortnightly or occasional subsidy to their welfare payments, but some people painted as many paintings as they needed until they had enough money for a big purchase like a car. When I first arrived, two old men had been a fixture in the town, sitting on their verandah every day, painting. When they had earned enough money to buy a truck for their outstation, they stopped.

As I stuck a documentation onto the back of each painting, I thought about the long journey these barks were on. They would have been painted, flat on the ground, perhaps on the verandah of Jack's house, with kids and dogs and dust surrounding them. (A well-known artist had once brought in a painting with his dog's footprints across it.) Then they would have been driven into town in an old four-wheel drive, wrapped in old blankets and sheets to protect them on the journey.

At the art centre we handled them carefully: we carried them by their edges, tried not to drop them, stacked them on foam supports. In the gallery where they would be exhibited, they would be handled with gloves on, several people allocated to carry each work around when it needed to be moved, always kept within a temperature-controlled environment. My work was part of this transformation: gluing the doco on the back of the bark was like adding a lens through which a Balanda could see it.

The docos converted a simple conversation with Jack into sophisticated and scholarly English, because that seemed like the best way to convey that the painting itself was sophisticated in its own culture. It seemed that writing about it in simple English would have implied that the painting itself was simplistic.

Each bark had my signature on the bottom, certifying its authenticity. In the world of Aboriginal art, a documented work is an authentic work, and authenticity has an almost reckonable commercial value. Maningrida was known for its high-quality documentations, so they were an important part of its trade. Over the years, so much media attention had been given to 'fake' Aboriginal paintings that art buyers now demanded a guarantee that the painting was genuine. The art centre certified that the painting was by a particular artist, with an implied guarantee that it was done by an Aboriginal person.

A small percentage of the artists represented by the centre were famous enough in Aboriginal art circles for their work to be sought after. These people had reputations, had been in numerous exhibitions and their work had been bought for high-profile collections. But the majority of the work was not 'fine art'. Providing a documentation for this type of work meant that it could be interpreted as a piece of another culture, as well as a piece of art. The explanations we wrote for these pieces underlined their foreignness, and enabled them to be sold as ethnographic curiosities to commercial galleries in Darwin, Sydney and Melbourne. This market promoted Aboriginal art as exotica, rather than as fine art. Some of this work also sold through tourist outlets, or directly from the art centre to relatives and friends of Balandas who came to visit the community.

The fine art was purchased by major museums and galleries, or sold through specialised commercial galleries like the one that was hosting Jack's exhibition. As I inverted my bottle of PVA glue over the back of the last painting I wondered why Aboriginal artists were called on to explain their work, and whether it was a good thing. Even though their work could be opaque to outsiders, was it so much more opaque than a non-Aboriginal abstract painting that it needed to be explained? Then again, I thought, it's a good way for Balandas to learn a bit about Aboriginal culture, and other contemporary artists do sometimes provide statements that accompany their work. Still I was conscious that 'authenticity'—whatever it means—had a special status in dealing with Aboriginal art. I had signed a note and stuck it to the bark declaring that it was by Jack. A redundant declaration, given that he had painted designs over which he had exclusive rights.

The guys carried the paintings out to the warehouse and began swathing them in cardboard to protect them on their journey. They would not be reading my painstaking documentations, because they knew the stories, they knew the country where the stories belonged, and they knew that these designs could only have been painted by one person.

∽ ∾

It was the season for spectacular artworks: the sap was running in the trees, making bark-harvesting much easier, and the plants for weaving were growing in profusion and easy to get. Berries for dying and sedge grasses to be made into baskets were only available in the Wet. Some plants were lush and malleable in the Wet, but hard and difficult to work with in the Dry. Something new and interesting was coming in every few days.

Charlie was one of the region's most famous artists. He and his wife, Lena, chartered a plane from Gamerdi, their outstation, to bring in a painting. It had been too big for the baggage compartment, so they had slid it into the cabin with the passengers, who held it propped against their fingers for the whole journey. At 3 metres by almost 2 metres, it was huge—and it was a masterpiece, a new interpretation of one of the themes

Charlie had been painting for years. It was too big for the storeroom, so Alice left it standing against the office wall. Any Balandas passing through the centre stopped to look, and others came in specially to see it. It had the kind of power possessed by only the greatest art and we were all mesmerised by it.

Sometimes when I was bored, confused or frustrated, I would go into one of the storerooms and look at the art. It was an uncomplicated pleasure to gaze on paintings, carvings, baskets and bags that were creative, unique, intriguing or simply well-crafted. It was a break from work and the philosophical doubts that sometimes shadowed my thoughts.

∽ ∾

Every day Jodie got under my skin, niggling away and irritating me until eventually I worked out why. She reminded me of myself when I had arrived in the community: idealistic, and wanting to help. She was in awe of Aboriginal people, her ideas about them revealing the kind of 'positive racism' that I had seen a lot in Maningrida. When she explained why she had wanted to come here, she talked about being fascinated by Aboriginal cultures, because the people were 'so spiritual'. Often, when I told people outside the community where I lived and worked, they had a similar reaction. From their knowledge of Dreamings and ceremony, they inferred that *all* Aboriginal people were richly spiritual. It made a change from the stereotype of the drunken no-hoper Aborigine, but it was still a simplistic way of looking at them. Like people anywhere, some Aboriginal people are more spiritual than others. It's true that someone's Dreaming permeates many facets of their life but it is as much related to identity, land ownership and family as it is to spirituality. Similarly, ceremonies are social gatherings as well as religious events, where people enjoy the music and the socialising in the same way that Balandas like parties.

My friend Stephanie was the same. She was the mother of a close friend of mine and planning to visit in the Dry. As we talked on the phone about where she should go and what she should see she said, 'I am prepared to be changed. I am prepared for the full-on spiritual connection to the land.' Surrounded by the spindly scrub of Arnhem Land, the smelly mangrove swamps, the forbidding rock country, I had forgotten that another one of the strongest messages that white urban Australia hears about Indigenous people is that they have a particular connection to the land. We assume that non-Indigenous people can somehow pick this special relationship up, and feel transported and transformed by 'Country', even though the Aboriginal connection to land is particular: it is their land, and it is a life-long relationship.

In Balanda thinking, Aboriginal people could be elevated and mythologised in a way that seemed to take away their status as real people. In the culture office, we had a special file where we kept strange requests from the outside world: researchers who wanted to explore the Aboriginal relationship with dolphins, or the spiritual dimensions of the didjeridu. I wondered if these ideas contributed to the white Australian tendency to patronise Aboriginal people, and to assume that problems in indigenous communities needed white Australian solutions.

Jodie said she was excited to be in Maningrida because Aboriginal society was so egalitarian—men and women had separate but equal spheres, and there was mutual respect, not like our patriarchal system. I thought of the domestic violence, the sexual violence; I thought of my own experience of harassment last December; I thought of Billie's wife, who kept her face averted while her husband spoke with his visitors; I thought of the fact that women used to lock themselves in the women's centre on wet weekends. I had seen so much evidence against the idea that men and women were equal in Aboriginal society that I had almost forgotten that these ideas existed. It struck me now as one of the many ways that white people romanticised Aboriginal people, attributing their own unrealised dreams to Aboriginal cultures.

But Jodie's ideas reminded me that I had come to Maningrida with similar romanticised perceptions, thinking that Aboriginal cultures and languages could remain intact, maybe even thrive, if only they were protected by a buffer of benevolent white people. I thought that it was appropriate for Balandas to do the work, because the role of 'being Aboriginal' was important and significant in itself, and should not be impinged on by Balanda-style work.

I had changed. Now I thought that our good intensions were patronising, and that our underlying assumptions about Aboriginal people reinforced their passive position and our right to make decisions on their behalf. I had come to be worried by the idea that Aboriginal people should be protected from our culture. Speaking to Jodie reminded me that in my first six months, my illusions had disappeared as I had struggled to make sense of the reality of community life. Even now, I was confused. I was able to rely on just one certainty when I grappled with the world I found myself in: the realisation that nothing was simple, that everything was paradoxical, that there were no clear answers.

Eight

THE WET SEASON TURNED THE DUSTY GROUND INTO MUD. I approached the art centre in leaps and tentative steps to avoid the mud and puddles. It was surrounded by a cloud of Glen 20, the sharp chemical smell seeping out into the air. Inside, Ricky and Samson were wearing gas masks and white gloves, treating sculptures and paintings for mould. Norris and Horace were bringing the pieces out of the storerooms and rearranging them according to their mould status. They were speaking Burarra and listening to Black American rap. Samson had started dressing differently from his friends. Instead of the standard floppy shorts and basketball tops, he now wore shiny black tracksuit pants with a black top, or red pants and a red top.

I was spending the week alone in my office, immersed in reading up on Aboriginal art, because the centre had been asked to write biographies of five of its artists for the *Oxford Companion to Aboriginal Art and Culture*. Part of the responsibility of the culture office was to provide information about the community to the outside world. My job was to interpret the cultures around me, and convert them into information. A lot of my work involved conscious or unconscious decisions about how Aboriginal people would be portrayed in a book, website, article, documentation or brochure that would probably be read by people with no other knowledge about Arnhem Land and the people who lived there.

All of the previous researchers had come to the job with a background in working with one of the local languages, so they brought some cultural knowledge to the position, and the ability to interview some of the artists in their own language. Because I didn't have this background, I relied on everything that had been left behind by the others—their draft dictionaries, their notes and their documentations. Luckily, because of my experience in a publishing house, I was surprisingly well qualified for the job.

The biographies would be published under my name, but most of the writing and information I produced went out under the name of Maningrida Arts & Culture, 'a community-based Aboriginal organisation'. The implication was that the views were those of the community, rather than the views of a rookie white woman fresh from Melbourne University. I tried to do the work responsibly. I didn't make anything up: I stuck to what could be verified. I was always conscious of avoiding representations that had the wrong feel, or a patronising tone, or seemed in some other way to be inappropriate. Sometimes this was all in a day's work, as easy as typing; at other times it seemed like a responsibility I had no right to.

We relied on the elaborate Balanda paraphernalia of information processing. Data was the lifeblood of the office, computer cables its veins and arteries, and the machines themselves were the vital organs. Aboriginal people had different ways of using and storing information. Having come only recently to writing systems, theirs is still fundamentally an oral culture. They had memories, songs, Dreamings, ceremony and their own voices.

The artists were already providing representations of their culture, in the form of paintings and sculpture, some of which was judged to be among the best of Australian contemporary art. To outsiders, the designs painted on bark with ochres are entirely cryptic: as cryptic, I think, as handwriting must have seemed to these artists' parents and grandparents when they saw it for the first time. In their world, the images made sense in complex but self-evident ways: they were about identity, and history, and spirituality, and law. Because outsiders were only able to skim the surface of meaning contained in the paintings, we relied on information about the paintings rather than the images themselves.

ᔕ ᔕ

Two weeks later, Samson came into my office.

'Can you teach me that computer?' he asked. 'I worked with Simon before. He teach me.'

My job often felt strangely isolated from the community, so I was pleased that he'd asked, and glad to have a chance to work more closely with one of the cedeepee staff. We started with what I was in the middle of doing—printing documentations from the database. We sat down at the computer together and I explained that there were sections for the artist's name, the subject of the artwork, the catalogue number, and the documentation. I showed Samson how to navigate the menus to find a particular entry, and then to print it. He picked it all up quickly, so I gave him a list of catalogue numbers and left him to print out the docos. It was the first time that a cedeepee worker had shown any interest in the computer. I wasn't sure what else I might be able to show Samson, but I decided to try to explain as much of the documentation process as possible.

A consultant had recently done a business plan for the centre, which recommended that a report should be produced each year. Alice had just finished writing the first one, and we wanted to make twenty copies to send out to various people. I showed Samson how to do this and how to use the spiral binding machine. He engaged Ricky as his assistant, and they spent the day in the culture office. As they worked, I could hear a stream of Burrara, gangsta-rap and Aboriginal English. I tuned in occasionally, and at one point I heard Samson say, 'I am *trouble*some nigger.' I was horrified by this phrase for a moment, then I felt stupid as I realised that it must have been lifted from one of the CDs they carried around with them.

ᗐ ᗏ

The bank queue never seemed to move. You could stand in the same spot for hours as people came in and out ahead of you. Its operation was opaque to outsiders, but Balandas seldom used the bank, which was administered by Bawinanga, because there was so little need for cash. In Melbourne, I had hardly ever left the house without my wallet, but in Maningrida, the only place for me to spend money was the shop, and I only went there once a fortnight.

But the bank was essential for Aboriginal people. There was a permanent line at the window, where Alan, one of Bawinanga's cedeepee staff, stood operating an eftpos machine. Alan was one of the older Aboriginal men who had been educated by missionaries, and sent away to Adelaide to go to school. He had excellent English, and the banking was no problem for him.

If he didn't come to work, there was mayhem. As the accountant for Bawinanga, Ron had to redeploy other people into the bank. Because so many of the cedeepee staff didn't have Alan's skill with numbers, he usually had to put one of the Balandas behind the counter, which meant that they got behind in their own work.

When Alan started staying away more than he was coming to work, Ron decided to leave the bank closed, and to explain to the angry queue that if they wanted it to open, they would have to go to Alan's house and talk to him about it. So they did. An hour later, Alan was standing in his place behind the window.

It was a simple step, but a conceptual revolution. Balanda staff always stepped in for cedeepee workers, and suddenly Ron was turning it back on them. The next day, he drew up a roster for eftpos duty. He understood that Alan was sick of it, so he put the cedeepee workers who were able to use the machine down for particular days each week. If they didn't turn up, he told the people who were waiting that it was Vicki's day or Daisy's day, and they went off to fetch their banker.

∽ ∾

We needed to have more photos of the women whose work would be featured in the weaving book. The work itself had been photographed by Balanda friends of Alice's from Melbourne. Maningrida was a town full of artists, people with an acute visual sensibility and an eye for composition. I thought maybe we could build on this instead of getting another Balanda in. I remembered the time I'd spent a few days in Darwin with a group of artists. One of them bought a polaroid camera at Cash Converters and had framed her cousins and aunts in the white plastic squares.

I asked the school whether it might be possible to run a photography project for some of the kids. The teenage boys had recently done a unit on rock music as part of the VET (Vocational Education and Training) program. I suggested that perhaps the girls could do a similar thing, taking photos of their relatives for the book. The teenage students were separated into boys' and girls' classes, to avoid putting together people who might be in a taboo cross-gender relationship with each other. For the same reason, the women featured in the book would have to be photographed by girls. The vice principal agreed that it was a good idea, and nominated Shane, a teacher, who was also a photographer, to supervise the project. He said he'd speak to Shane and tell him to speak to me.

∽ ∾

Samson came into the culture office a couple of times a week. He took to calling me 'gapala', a term of respect for an older person. Although he thought I was much older than him, he was joking about the respect, so I called him 'gapala' in return. In fact we were almost the same age, both in our mid-twenties. I thought about what I could teach him to do: the functions of the database were simple enough, and Samson was smart, so I had no doubt that he could use and understand the computer. But the data itself was all in English. Samson's English was relatively good, but it had been learnt at school and in Maningrida, so it only went so far. I started to put aside the computer-related jobs that I thought he could do so that there was work for him when he came in—printing out artist CVs or documentations, or entering information from exhibition catalogues into artist CVs. Sometimes, if the work had to be done immediately, I would go and find Samson in the warehouse and ask if he could come and do the task.

While most of the Aboriginal people in Maningrida were tolerant of Balandas, Samson was actively interested in Balanda life and culture. There was a story that as a kid he sometimes broke into Balanda houses—not to steal anything, but just to look around. He asked questions all the time, unlike most Aboriginal people who answered questions about their culture, but didn't usually ask about Balanda culture. Samson was interested in computers because he was bored with packing and cleaning, but also because they were part of the Balanda world.

One day, I suggested that he could teach me his language, Burarra, but he wasn't keen.

'You read that book,' he said, referring to the 700-page English/Burarra dictionary.

'I can't learn by reading the book!' I said.

'Yo, it's all in that book, you read it and you will learn.'

This was the problem with learning a language in Maningrida: you had to ask a speaker for a lot of their time and patience. I wasn't surprised that Samson wasn't interested in teaching me, but I did catch the odd word here and there as we worked together.

∽ ∾

When I had been working with Samson for a few days, Horace came in and said, 'Can you show me that computer?' I said yes, of course—but I soon found that Horace could neither read nor write more than his own name. I hadn't thought before about how much computers rely on literacy: all of the commands on the menus on the database program were words. If I explained that he had to go to 'find' and click there, he wouldn't know what the word 'find' looked like.

We had to go right back to basics—Horace hadn't used a keyboard or a mouse before. I wrote his name on a piece of paper, and he typed it painstakingly, one letter at a time. He moved the mouse erratically, finally learning that its movement corresponded to the position of the arrow on the screen. After an hour he leapt up and said, 'I come back to tomorrow,' and sauntered out of the room.

I was keenly aware that I wasn't qualified or experienced to teach basic computer skills, let alone literacy. Samson had enough knowledge to be able to pick up computer skills quickly, but Horace was starting from the very beginning. He didn't understand that the computer was a tool that we used to produce documentations, to send emails and to control the stock. From the outside, it looked like using the computer was a task in itself, a mysterious labour that Balandas devoted themselves to. Horace wasn't aware that the skills he needed to use the computer went far beyond knowing which button to press and how to use the mouse. I was daunted by his lack of knowledge, and I didn't know where to begin. At the same time, I had other work to do, and there was a limit to how much time I could put in to training

Horace. And yet, I felt that if these young men wanted to learn, then I should be prepared to teach them.

Horace came back a couple of days later. I wrote out a sentence for him to type. When this was done, we printed it. He was happy with his achievement. It had taken almost an hour, but he had a printed piece of paper in his hand.

At the end of the week, Horace left to go off for ceremony. I was guiltily relieved that I had escaped having to find more ways to teach him.

∽ ∾

I was going to Melbourne for five days for the wedding. The man who had harassed me in December had not come back, and I had felt safe since returning to Maningrida. I bought a return ticket and as I made this decision, I began to wonder how long I would stay. I still struggled to understand Maningrida and my place in it. I had lost my illusions about Aboriginal communities, but I wanted to turn the confusion I felt into a coherent understanding. I kept thinking that if only I thought about it hard enough, everything would become clear and I could find solutions to the problems that surrounded me.

I stood at the sink doing the dishes the night before my trip, thinking about why I had come to Maningrida in the first place. I had wanted to do a job that had a positive impact on the world; I knew that I didn't want to work for some big corporation, and

I was bored with my job in academic publishing. I wanted to orient my life in a direction that might help other people.

By now, such a simple idea seemed embarrassingly naïve. Now I had no idea whether the work I did was any use. It wasn't a question of the work being 'good' or 'bad'—we were simply required to take our places in the big Balanda machine. If I left, someone else would come along and do the same job.

I didn't see a future for myself in this 'Aboriginal industry'. I needed to think about what I wanted to do, rather than what I ought to do as dictated by my strong but unfocussed social conscience. I had never really had a desire to pursue a career for its own sake; I had fallen into my previous job in publishing almost accidentally, and hadn't had any better ideas until I decided to go Maningrida. I had lots of skills and experience, but I had no direction.

I finished the dishes, packed my bag and got everything ready for my trip. I realised that at some point I would leave permanently. When would that be, and where would I be going?

～ ～

When I got back in the middle of March, Archie mentioned that I would need to provide a budget for the language project at the end of the financial year so that ATSIC would release the funds for the next year. I was confused.

'Don't we automatically get the second lot of funding?'

'No. They want to make sure that we've spent the first lot before they'll give us any more!' He was laughing at me. 'Otherwise it looks like we didn't need the money, and they'll find someone else to give it to.'

Most of the linguists I had contacted had said that they were interested in the project, but would prefer to come in the second year. I had assumed that this would be fine, but now it seemed that I had three months to spend $95,000—or the centre would lose the funding.

I put the weaving book aside and spent days re-organising the project. I needed to have the money spent, or firmly committed with a purchase order. And for some of the budget items I needed to get three quotes, and then choose the cheapest or give a good explanation for why I would be choosing a different one. I was constantly anxious that I would not be able to get everything done on time, and that the project would fail because of me.

Samson came in a couple of times, hoping to work on the computer, but I was too busy working on the budget to help him. I had investigated computer training courses for him, but there was nothing in Maningrida—he would have to go to Darwin. It was unthinkable for someone like him to sacrifice living with his family, within his own language and culture, and near his country, all for the sake of computer skills. I just hoped he would still be interested in working in the culture office when I was free again in a couple of weeks.

∾ ∾

My first visitor from the south arrived as the Dry was setting in. Stephanie, my friend's mother, was a mother figure to me as well. She brought a Styrofoam box full of 'city food' and a fresh copy of the *Age*.

I took her on a tour of the art centre, the museum and Bawinanga. As we left the office, she said, 'What would happen if someone actually picked up the rubbish?'

'What rubbish?' I asked.

'The rubbish that's everywhere, all over the ground?'

I looked around me, and saw that the ground was covered with old chip packets, pie packets, drink bottles, take-away food bags and anonymous pieces of paper and plastic—the rubbish had also struck me when I first arrived but now I no longer noticed it. I thought about her question.

'It would probably come back. Kids would come and turn over the rubbish bins again, and people would keep throwing their rubbish on the ground. Every so often cedeepee do a clean up, but it's pretty much always here.'

I took Stephanie to the shop on Saturday morning, curious about what it would look like to an outsider. By now I was used the throngs of people, the mangy dogs wandering around and the prices. Stephanie reacted the way I did the first time: she was struck by the heavy wire mesh everywhere, by the poor quality of the fruit and vegetables and by the colonial-era feel to the stock: the biggest sections were for 5-kilo tins of white sugar, 2-kilo packets of white flour, tea and powdered milk. The freezer had a few frozen meals, some desserts and large packages of meat—mainly chops, sausages and mince meat, with a few kangaroo tails—30 or 40-centimetre sections, butchered just like the other meat and shrink-wrapped onto black plastic trays. We bought milk and eggs. Everything else I had ordered from Darwin.

As we walked home, she commented on the fact that it had seemed that we were invisible to the Aboriginal people in the shop. It was full, as always on a Saturday morning, but no-one said hello, or smiled or acknowledged our presence. This was familiar to me by now; it was part of the social and cultural separation in the town. I was only greeted by people who knew me well, even though I was aware that nearly everybody in the shop would know who I was, where I lived and where I worked.

I had noticed that the Aboriginal people in Maningrida didn't seem to have a place for small talk and making conversation for the sake of politeness alone. I thought about the reason for this. Balandas live in relatively big communities full of people we don't know very well, if at all, so we rely on certain phrases to create and maintain casual relationships. In a shop, we usually have a little conversation with the salesperson: hello, how are you? Well, thanks. Aboriginal people didn't seem to bother with this. At first, when I interviewed artists, I expected them to do the polite, Balanda, hello-how-are-you preamble, but they tended to get straight to the point.

I speculated that because Aboriginal people had traditionally lived in small societies, they perhaps didn't need the kind of politeness that creates a temporary relationship with a stranger. They had an etiquette of their own, which I must have unwittingly violated all the time. And because everyone in Aboriginal societies had a skin name, and a nominated place in the social universe, it made sense to me that they perhaps had no need for the waffle Balandas use to create and maintain relationships with strangers, colleagues or acquaintances.

The weather had been better, the humidity finally drying out after months of damp air, but it was still too humid for Stephanie, straight from Melbourne's cool dry autumn. The hot days brought the kids out at night, when it was cooler. They played in the schoolyard, running, screaming, climbing over buildings and calling out to each other. My flat was so close to the school that I could hear it all. They had recently taken to whistling, an elaborate system of so many different sounds that it seemed they had created a code. Part of me was impressed, but as Stephanie and I lay in bed after midnight with their squeals and whistles keeping us awake, I couldn't help wishing they would all go home to bed.

Stephanie was incredulous. 'Don't they have homes to go to? What do their parents think of them running wild so late at night? Why doesn't an adult come and get them?'

Once again, I realised that this was an aspect of Maningrida life that I had become accustomed to: children were not disciplined in the way they were in Balanda culture. They were often left to their own devices. This made them independent, confident, often cheeky—I was almost always impressed by the way they interacted with me—but, at the same time, they were left to run wild, and they were not sent to school. Letterboxes, rubbish bins and gardens were vandalised so often that it was not even commented on. I imagined that the independence of children worked better out in the bush, and that it was yet another aspect of traditional culture that had not translated well to the town.

⁓ ⁓

It was Stephanie's last day, and I took her to the airport. I asked whether she'd enjoyed her visit. She was glad she'd come, she said, but she'd found it educational and eye-opening rather than enjoyable. Maningrida had become normal enough for me that it hadn't occurred to me to prepare her for the culture shock, the poverty, the heat, the unruly children and the dogs. She confessed she'd ended up feeling exhausted by it all.

'I felt more at home in Europe,' she said. 'I remember when I was in Prague—I couldn't speak the language or read the street signs. But at least I could "read" the culture.'

In Maningrida, she told me, she couldn't make sense of what she saw, and she felt overwhelmed by the foreignness and the conditions in which Aboriginal people lived. For Stephanie, being in Maningrida was like being in the bank queue for me: I didn't understand how it worked, and when people came in ahead of me, I didn't know if they were jumping the queue, or if they were following their own rules with people holding places for them. The Aboriginal people in the line didn't make allowances—they either assumed that I knew how it worked, or didn't think they needed to look after me. I had learnt, little by little, enough to feel more at home in Maningrida, but part of what I had learnt was how to live with the feeling of being somewhere utterly foreign, and often incomprehensible.

Back at work I began organising a Rembarrnga spelling conference. There were enough materials to write the dictionary and learner's guide for this language, but it was complicated by the fact that there were two different ways of spelling it. The Rembarrnga people had been spread out over Arnhem Land, and there were now two communities—a southern and a northern. Different linguists and teachers had worked with the community over the years, and now the language was spelled differently in the north and the south. We needed to get the whole community together to decide which system should be used in the dictionary.

We decided to fly the southern mob up to Maningrida for three days in June. The project linguist had contacted people he knew in the south, and they had agreed to come along and to spread the word. Now I needed to organise a venue, catering, charter flights and accommodation. I also needed to book travel for two linguists: one was coming in May to work on Nakara, spoken just east of Maningrida, and another was coming in June to work on Djinang, Elroy's language.

There were also some documentations to do, so I asked Samson if he would like to help. Some of them were straightforward: he just needed to copy the text out of an old document into a new document, and enter the artist's name and the catalogue number of the work.

Then Alice brought in a painting that needed some new information added to the documentation. Instead of doing it myself, I decided to try to help Samson to add the new information. I was so used to writing in English, and in the particular style that seemed right for a quasi-scholarly documentation, that it was difficult for me to hold back and let Samson write the information in his own words.

This task proved to be much more difficult than any of the other work we had done together. Samson's English and literacy were both excellent by Maningrida standards, but he would hardly ever have written in English. He stalled again and again, asking me whether this word or that word would be the right one. Finally, he had written the three sentences that the documentation needed. I read over them and checked the spelling, and we printed it out. This had been really hard work for Samson; it was no longer fun.

He left for the day and I read over his sentences. The meaning was clear, but they were written in Aboriginal English. Any Balanda reading this would see it as ungrammatical and uneducated. My instinct was to 'fix' his work, but as I sat holding the piece of paper I realised that changing his words to standard English would be imposing yet another layer of Balanda on Samson's culture. Was the role of the centre to make Aboriginal art and culture as digestible as possible for non-Aboriginal people? What would the gallery think if I left the doco as it was? Samson had laboured for ages to produce this. He was probably exhausted. So was I. I put the paper down and tried to go back to my other work, but I couldn't concentrate.

Samson didn't come back to the culture office for the rest of the week, and I spent each day feeling that I was failing. I felt I was failing Samson but, more than that, I felt all of us Balandas, with our Balanda systems and ways, were failing the community we worked for. If Samson, one of the smartest and most literate young men in the community, was fundamentally excluded from the work being done in the cultural research office, then what did that say about the work we did? The concepts and culture of the kind of work I did were alien—irrelevant even—to Samson, and so were the skills the work needed. I wanted to bridge the gap between my work and him, but I had no idea how to do it. He was too smart to continue packing artwork and cleaning shelves. The next week, he only came to work twice, and didn't come into the culture office either time.

∽ ∾

I hadn't heard anything from the vice principal or Shane about the photography idea, so when I happened to see Shane in the art centre one day I asked him about it. The vice principal hadn't mentioned anything to him, so I explained my idea.

'No way,' he said. 'It just wouldn't work. The kids would only be into it for a few minutes, and they wouldn't be careful enough, and it would end up being yours truly who would have to take the photos himself. Sorry.'

I said that the photos wouldn't have to be perfect—just well-lit, so that people's faces didn't disappear into black splodges. He explained his opposition to the plan at more length, making it a diatribe on my ignorance. Every word whispered, 'I've been here longer than you and I know.' I had come across this attitude before: the inert conviction that nothing would work. Shane might have been right: he was a teacher, and had much more experience than me. But I resented him patronising me, and I resented the fact that he said no without giving it a second's thought.

He left me deflated. I would have to do it the usual way, by flying in a Balanda photographer from Darwin.

As Shane left I heard the phone ringing, and went into the arts office to answer it. For a moment my spirits lifted as I heard Valerie on the line; then, as she greeted me, I heard the drunken slur in her voice and disappointment set in. 'Yabok,' she said. 'You my sister, belinj, yabok.' Then her voice went quiet. 'Yabok, you give me some hundred dollar?'

'No, sorry Valerie, but I don't have any money.'

'Oh, yabok, you can help me . . .' Her words dissolved into giggles, growing into peals of laughter.

I knew it was unreasonable, but I felt let down by her. I had wanted her to be someone I could get to know, and instead she had become an annoying voice humbugging me on the phone from Darwin.

She came back on the line and said, 'Just one hundred dollar for your sister, yabok, yabok?'

I tried to keep the frustration out of my voice as I refused again. As calmly as I could, I said goodbye and put the phone down. What would become of her if she stayed in Darwin drinking cheap moselle every day? And what would become of her if she came home?

∽ ∾

By the time the footy grand final came around in the middle of April, Samson had stopped coming to the art centre completely. Frustrated Balandas often complained about the lack of commitment on the part of cedeepee staff, and it was certainly true that a Balanda work ethic was not part of their culture. But, as I learnt with Samson, it was much more complicated than that. And it was a kind of complication that felt unbridgeable.

The Yilan team didn't make it into the grand final, but we all planned to go and watch the match anyway. The Crocodiles and the Crows had made it through; Ricky told me to support the Crocodiles, so I did.

It was a typical 'Build Down' day—the opposite to the Build Up—the weather was drier and finer all the time, but it hadn't dried out completely, so it was still fairly humid and with a chance of rain. The Balandas took tarps, umbrellas and eskies to the football oval and settled in. I looked around. It was an unremarkable open space in the town, usually covered with rubbish, fairly empty, with perhaps a few people strolling around it to get to Side Camp or the school. Today, the whole town had turned out. People had painted their faces in their team's colours, and there was even a car that had been painted yellow and black for the Crocodiles. It was parked near the scoreboard, bursting with fans dressed and coated in yellow and black.

I knew there would sometimes be big ceremonies that brought many Aboriginal people together, but this was the only time I saw the whole community—Balanda and Aboriginal—together. I hadn't followed the footy season, but today the excitement was palpable.

It began with the cheer squads coming out onto the field. The teenage girls' class at the school had been practising all week. They were dressed in perfectly coordinated outfits with pom poms, an incredible sight in a community uniformly dressed in faded, floppy cotton. They performed modest, sedate, but carefully choreographed routines to pop songs, and then left the field.

Then the two huge banners came out, one with the Crows' insignia, and one for the Crocodiles. I was incredulous. Most of the time it seemed that the Aboriginal community was oblivious to Balanda concerns, but today they had captured every detail of this elaborate Balanda ritual perfectly. The teams ran out, thirty-six men perfectly dressed in new uniforms and taut knee-length socks. Finally, the umpires, flown in specially from Darwin for the day, emerged. Since a riot had broken out at the end of a grand final a few years before, the umpires were now escorted to and from the field by police.

The excitement gradually ebbed as the Crows defeated the Crocodiles soundly. The community was divided according to footy team, but for once the division wasn't between Aboriginal and Balanda. And it was a unified event: we were all there for the footy, brought together by its spectacular finale.

Inspiration was in the air; Mal was talking about teaching numbers and addition via a football scoreboard. I was also struck by the number of young men who had turned up. What did they do for the rest of the week—and the rest of the year? They weren't all working in cedeepee jobs—the program wasn't big enough. Some would go back to their outstations for the Dry. Others would stay, absorbed into the growing town-based culture.

∾ ∾

I thought a lot about why cedeepee workers stopped coming to the centre, and I wondered whether partly it was because they didn't feel valued or needed—after all, they tended to have very little responsibility. I decided to go and visit Samson, to tell him that we missed him and would like him to come to work again. Norris told me he was staying at 'that green downstairs house' in the old part of town. I drove over there one afternoon. I got out of the truck and called out. 'Hello! Samson! Hello!'

It took several minutes for him to emerge. His shoulders were hunched over; he was wearing shorts, rather than his usual carefully composed outfits, and his face was thick with sleep and ganja.

'Hello, gapala,' he said.

'Hello, Gun-mala?' I said, although I could see he was clearly not good. 'I just wanted to see how you're going.'

'I'm sick,' he said, coughing.

I explained that we missed him and would like him to come back, and that there was plenty of work for him to do. He said he would come back when his cough was better. I wished him well and told him to take care of himself. Then with a cheery 'See ya,' I got in the car and drove off.

I knew that he wasn't going to come back. I knew he was asleep in the afternoon because he'd been up all night smoking ganja, and that his cough was a smoker's cough.

I drove back to work with frustration and sadness welling up inside me. I had done what I could, and it was so very little.

Nine

WITHIN A WEEK OF SAMSON'S DEPARTURE, TWO NEW WORKERS had arrived. People enrolled on the cedeepee program chose which agency to work for, so like all the other workers before them, Janey and Chelsea simply turned up one day. They were the first women to have chosen this option since I had started there. Most cedeepee jobs were done by men—the town maintenance crew, the rangers, the builders and the mud-brick factory workers were all male. There was also a special women's cedeepee program, with jobs at the women's centre, which was a hub for childcare, meals on wheels and other family-oriented work.

Janey and Chelsea were about sixteen, and the art centre seemed like a good choice for them. As short, slight, teenage girls, it was unlikely they would want to do the physical labour involved in most of the cedeepee jobs. When Alice introduced us, Janey said, 'Hi, how are you?' and I immediately noticed that her English was very lightly accented. It turned out that she had a non-Aboriginal parent, and had grown up in Darwin and recently moved to Maningrida. She switched easily between fluent Balanda English and fluent Aboriginal English.

I tended to notice the English level of Aboriginal people when I met them. Although there were cultural differences as well as language differences, it seemed possible to bridge the cultural gap with enough shared language. Because I didn't speak any of the local languages, this meant relying on Aboriginal people to speak enough English to communicate with me. It wasn't possible to learn a few words from each person, slowly building up enough phrases to have a simple conversation, because everyone I spoke to had different languages. Balandas who worked closely with one or two Aboriginal people could do this more easily, but I talked to artists from all of the language groups, and although the arts workers tended to be Burarra speakers, I seldom worked closely enough with them to pick up much of their language.

This was limiting for me because I wanted to talk about their culture, ask them what they thought about Balandas and talk about Maningrida. But even with Valerie and Samson, any attempts at a more complex conversation would stall as they frowned in confusion at the English words they didn't know, or simply shrugged the question off, moving back to the common ground of jokes and chat.

During the week, Denise from the school came in asking for submissions to a community newspaper they were putting together. It was called the *Manayingkarírra Djúrrang*, the 'Maningrida paper'.

'They used to do a paper every few months, and we've decided to get it going again,' she said. 'We're just asking everyone for a couple of hundred words on what they're doing, and photos if you have them. We really want to have lots of pictures and not too much text.'

When I came out of my office later in the morning I saw Janey taking photos of Elroy and Chelsea, as well as photographing some paintings, with the new digital camera. When we bought the camera we had chosen the simplest model, so that the workers could be trained to use it quickly and easily. But still, I had expected that most of the photos, which were used for the archive or to email to potential buyers and exhibitors, would be taken by Balandas. I thought of the short-lived plan to have the school students take photos for the weaving book, and felt my frustration with Shane return. But I had to admit that Janey wasn't the average Maningrida teenager.

It was usually my job to write anything produced by the centre, but Janey volunteered to write the article to go with the images for the newspaper. She asked Alice what it should cover, and then wrote about our new website and the artists who had recently gone to Sydney for their exhibitions.

It was tempting to think that Janey's experience in the Balanda world would make her an ideal staff member. But we had been impressed by George and Samson as well. I had learnt to be wary òf expecting too much of new workers.

                ∽ ∾

I was talking to Thelma outside the JET Centre when Nellie came up. She waited for us to finish our conversation, and then we sat on the bench outside and began our usual exchange of words. But this time I wasn't sure what she was saying. After she had repeated herself a couple of times, I decided to pretend to understand—I had learnt that with people I found hard to understand, the meaning would often emerge as a conversation progressed. A group of people walked by, and suddenly Nellie was saying something about a dead body—and then she began to wail. She rocked back and forth and wept, and through her wailing came a kind of chanting I couldn't decipher. Mal came out to see whether everything was all right. I sat there, not knowing what to do. Did she want to be comforted? Should I touch her, or leave her to cry in peace? Should I stay with her, or go away? Why was she crying like this?

Mal whispered to me over Nellie's bent head: 'I asked Thelma and she says it's OK, she's just grieving. Just go with it.'

OK, I thought, but I felt awkward and out of place as I sat next to Nellie and her outpouring of emotion. After a few minutes—intense minutes fraught with pain—she stopped and we talked about her sadness in four or five of the English words we shared. She tried to tell me who had died, but I was no wiser, her words lost in a maze of obscure references to the dead person I didn't know, who in Nellie's culture could not be named.

∽ ∾

I went to the airport to collect a visiting art buyer, and was surprised to see a group of old women there painted with white ochre. Then I realised they were a funeral party, waiting to receive a body. When the body arrived it was greeted with singing and dancing before being driven to the house where the funeral was being held. I recognised Nellie in the group of women.

Later, I found out that the woman who had died was one of the traditional owners of the Maningrida land. The funeral was held at one of the houses near the shop. As usual, the family had barricaded the road, the area around the house had been cleared of rubbish and raked smooth, and a bush shelter had been erected for the body.

The Balandas were invited to the first day of the funeral. It began with Christian songs and dancing by a group of young women and girls, all dressed in white. Like all Christian music in Maningrida, the hymns were more like pop music than church music, with lyrics like 'Jesus put 'im higher, higher higher higher; devil put 'im lower, lower lower lower'. The hymns were sung karaoke-style, to a backing tape.

Then came the Aboriginal songs. A group of men sat to one side with clapsticks and didjeridus, playing the right songs for the old woman who had died. I recognised Samson among the dancers. He was known as a master dancer, and at last I could see why. With the earring gone, and his skin covered in white ochre, dressed in a naga (loincloth), he looked for once just like the other young men around him. But he stood out because of his evocative, elegant movements and perfectly timed steps, these skills the only hint of the Samson I knew, the flashy exhibitionist. It reminded me that I couldn't judge Samson's life or overall wellbeing by the fact that he had left the art centre. Perhaps in his own world he was as functional, happy and confident as ever.

We stayed for a few hours, sitting in the sun watching the dancing, or just waiting for the next thing to happen. These ceremonies were unhurried and would go on for about a week before the final burial.

I hadn't been to a funeral in Maningrida before, although I was often aware of them. I knew that there were times of intense emotion, where women would wail and scream, flagellating themselves with stones and tearing at their hair and clothes. But today's ceremonies were partly a cultural performance. It was the open Balanda day; the real business of mourning would begin the next day as the family took over and moved into their private grief.

ॐ ॐ

Nellie came in to see me the week after the funeral, all smiles and toothless words, and we had our usual chat. I showed her my new book on contemporary basketry from around the world, thinking that she might be interested in other kinds of baskets, as well as seeing her own work in a book like this. She laughed at pictures of baskets made from distorted twigs and plastics and wire. When she came to a photo of a man weaving a basket she thought it was hilarious, and made the sound the old women made when something cheeky was going on: a long, drawn out rising tone. She crowed in a mixture of shyness and pride when she found the photo of her and her work. We were managing a kind of communication with pictures and sounds, if not with words.

Nellie was old enough to remember the arrival of the first Balanda. She had grown up in the bush and learnt the traditional weaving techniques, making dilly bags and conical mats in plain pandanus. Those early Balandas had suggested the women make their mats flat instead of domed, and that they dye the pandanus instead of leaving it in its natural colour, to make their work more saleable for the Balanda market in the city. Now it was extremely rare for anything made of undyed pandanus to come in to the art centre. Nellie had grown up making baskets to use, and now she made baskets to sell. I wondered what other changes she had seen, and what she thought about the Balandas in Maningrida and how her children and grandchildren now lived. But, frustratingly, this remained one of the many things we didn't have enough shared words to discuss.

༅ ༅

Alice and I decided that I should accompany three Kuninjku women to Sydney for the opening of an exhibition of their screenprints and etchings. This was normally Alice's job, but she had been away from Maningrida twice in a few weeks and wanted me to go instead. I was excited about it, looking forward to spending more time with Maisie, Nancy and Valerie. I had got to know them the previous year, while writing documentations of their prints. But I was worried about Valerie, who had just come back from five months' drinking.

I was shocked when I saw her: her usually confident stance had changed to a cowed look, her head bowed. Her forehead had a huge gash across it, apparently the legacy of a drunken fight with her sister. The police, the hospital and this fight were all mentioned in the same sentence.

We were supposed to be leaving in a couple of weeks. I looked at the frail, pale version of who Valerie used to be, and thought about all the things that could go horribly wrong in Sydney if her desire for grog was stronger than her desire to . . . behave herself? Act appropriately? Be like the rest of us? I wasn't clear about exactly what I wanted from her, but I was clear about my fear of being responsible for her if she went on a bender in a strange city.

A couple of weeks passed, and Valerie dried out, became healthier and started producing some art. She seemed to emerge from a shrunken version of herself: once again she was walking into my office for a chat, her huge smile glowing in her beautiful face. Gradually, my old affection for her replaced the frustration I'd been feeling. Each time she came in she seemed more like herself.

Then there was a wet weekend, and Amos, her husband, bashed her. The next time I saw her she was wearing a plaster cast on her left arm, looking bruised.

I was upset, knowing that I was powerless to protect her. But at least she would have five days' respite in Sydney, where she would be too far away for her husband to get at her.

∾ ∾

At 7 o'clock I was on a flight to Sydney with Nancy, Maisie and Valerie. Nancy, known as Valerie's mother—in Balanda terms her aunt—was a woman of about sixty who had lived all her life in the bush with only occasional trips into Maningrida. She had unruly, wiry grey-white hair, stained an orangey-brown at the front by nicotine. She spoke very little English, and her voice was raspy from years of cigarettes. Maisie was thin with lush, loosely curly hair. She was an assistant teacher at their outstation school, and was married to one of Valerie's brothers. Valerie was the spokeswoman of the group—the most outgoing, and the most confident with Balandas, even though Maisie's English was equally good.

As soon as we had taken off, Valerie tried to order a rum and Coke from the flight attendant. I was desperately hoping that she wouldn't use Sydney as the opportunity for another binge, and was relieved that she didn't have the $5 for the drink. I pretended not to have any money either.

We were staying in a serviced apartment, so on our first morning we had breakfast there. Nancy sat at the table and barked out instructions to the younger women; she never made her own tea, or got her own breakfast. It seemed to be understood that they had a duty to look after her.

The women were all shocked by the cold, and had put on every garment they had with them. Our first priority was buying warm clothes. We caught the monorail from Darling Harbour into the city to go shopping. Here, we were confronted with an escalator. Nancy had never used one before, and as an older woman, unsteady on her legs at the best of times and suffering from a problem with her right knee, she found it difficult. I took her arm and stepped on and off the disappearing steps in time with her. The others were more confident, but still wary.

For them, Sydney—'the big city'—was a constant adventure. It was full of people and things they found hilarious, shocking or bizarre. It was the opposite of Maningrida: instead of being in the Balanda minority, I was part of the dominant culture, and the women, used to being in the majority, were outsiders. They stayed close together, and close to me: the city was a huge, disorienting beast and they did not want to get lost in it.

When the women were approached by a waiter or a shop assistant, they would call me over: 'Helen!' their corruption of my name, or 'Belinj!' I did all the talking: I bought the tickets for the monorail, paid for the clothes, bought cigarettes, asked for directions. I remembered my experience at Korlobidadah, feeling amazed that Leo and Isaac could not only find their way around terrain that looked inhospitable to me, but could survive and prosper there. Although they were relying on me to navigate the city for them, Nancy, Maisie and Valerie would have more chance of surviving in Sydney than I would have had in the remote reaches of Arnhem Land, because they had been to Darwin and seen enough of Balanda culture to have some idea about it.

Once everybody had a warm outfit—socks, jeans, warm skirts and big flannelette jackets—we had lunch in a food court. I was longing for a fresh salad sandwich after months of wilted vegetables but the others headed straight for the deep-fried chicken and chips. We stopped in the afternoon for a cup of tea in a café; our four days in Sydney would be constantly punctuated by tea drinking. They recreated bush tea by sloshing in generous amounts of milk, and emptying at least four little sachets of sugar into each cup. I ordered coffee, sipping each glass slowly and appreciatively. Whenever we were sitting around like this, I would try to learn some Kuninjku. I asked the words for sugar, tea and water. Maisie, a teacher, insisted that I get out my notebook and write them down. Then I tried to repeat them back, invariably mangling the sounds, to a chorus of laughter. They leant forward and repeated the words loudly and slowly until finally I got them nearly right. Eventually I learnt to say 'karri-re'—'we're going' or 'let's go'.

On our way to the exhibition opening that night, we met my friend James for a drink in a large, renovated inner city pub. I was anxious about Nancy not getting a seat in the crowded bar, but I needn't have worried. We went to the back and asked two men sitting on a couch whether we could take the surrounding chairs. They agreed but within minutes got up, leaving all the seats to us. It seemed to be done out of respect. After our drink we made our way through the front bar. The crowd parted for us. People were standing back for the Aborigines. I wondered why. Was it because the sight of three women with skin like rich dark velvet was so unusual? James, who walked behind us, observed people's reactions. They were obviously surprised and didn't quite know where to look. One of them made eye contact with him, expecting him to share her moment of disorientation, but her expression changed when she saw that James was with us.

James and I made jokes about people standing aside as their effort for reconciliation. I suppose these jokes were about our sense of superiority. But I knew that if I had been in that bar a year before, my own medley of white guilt, ignorance and earnest but unfocussed respect would probably have made me act the same way. We had attracted attention all day, because the women were so distinctive—not only for their dark skin, but also for their hair, their demeanour and the way they were dressed.

At the opening, Nancy, Maisie and Valerie were the focus of attention, with nearly everyone from the Sydney art world wanting to be introduced to them. Most of these conversations stalled when the English ran out; at that point, the Balandas often turned to me. One woman told me a story about her holiday in northern Queensland.

'We were on the ferry and a little community of Aboriginal children got on. I had never seen Aboriginal children before, and they were just wonderful—so unspoilt, and innocent, you know?'

I kept my responses vague—'Right, yeah'—thinking of the kids in Maningrida who could be many things, from adorable to destructive, but were seldom innocent.

A man who worked in an Aboriginal art gallery told me that it was a privilege for him to meet the women, 'because theirs is such a truly spiritual culture'.

I said, 'Well, I don't know if you can call a whole culture spiritual,' my gaze following Valerie as she accepted another glass of white wine. I decided to get her an orange juice to slow her down a bit.

A year living in Maningrida had changed my thinking about Aboriginal people: they had become real flesh and blood people to me rather than stereotypes of the spiritual.

From this perspective, it seemed to me that the reactions Valerie and the others were getting in Sydney were something akin to racism. It wasn't the traditional white Australian racism, which treats Aboriginal people as one category and then makes negative assumptions about that category. It was the same process reversed: blanket positive assumptions made about Aboriginal people in the name of respect.

I had always thought of Maningrida as utterly unlike the city; the Balanda culture there had so many differences from mainstream Australian culture. But it struck me now that Balandas often made patronising assumptions about Aboriginal people, whether they were in Sydney or in Maningrida. I saw similarities between the belief I'd seen in Balandas who worked in Aboriginal communities (that Aboriginal people are not capable of interpreting and understanding Balanda culture without sacrificing their own culture) and the attitude I was seeing in Sydney (that all Aboriginal people are worthy of respect, not for who they are or what they do, but simply for being Aboriginal).

∾ ∾

Having finished our official duties, the next day we became tourists. We went to the Museum of Contemporary Art, where there was an exhibition of bark paintings and sculpture from Maningrida. As we looked, we realised that the women were related to most of the artists in that exhibition. It struck me that these women came from an incredibly talented family—their own work was impressive, and they were in a huge room full of stunning work by their relatives. There was a disproportionately high number of successful artists in that family.

As relatives, the women were given special permission to take photographs. The art looked incredible in this context: I had seen similar work nearly every day in Maningrida, stacked on shelves, or leaning against walls surrounded by hundreds of other pieces. But in the gallery, surrounded by clear space and white walls, it was much more impressive. It was beautiful, abstract, captivating; the sculptures of spirit figures were charming, and also intriguing, with patterns of dots and lines painted on their chests that hinted at identity and ceremony. The bark paintings shimmered with the effect they are famous for, a kind of optical illusion created by the density of so many fine lines of cross-hatching.

But Nancy, Maisie and Valerie were much more interested in their relationships to the artists than the work itself. They were proud of their sons, cousins and brothers for being on show in Sydney, but the designs were so familiar to them that they didn't need to take time to look at them.

By contrast, the other visitors stood for long minutes in front of the paintings and leant forward to get as close as they could to the sculptures. They walked around with the quiet steps reserved for galleries, libraries and churches, taking their time to appreciate the work.

As we left, Maisie began to nag me about going to Darwin. They were flying back there early on Saturday morning, with a connecting flight booked to Maningrida. Maisie had decided that she wanted to stay in Darwin to visit a relative who was in hospital. I could see why Maisie wanted to visit him but I was worried about Valerie ending up in the city again. She had dried out so recently that I thought it would probably be a temptation for her. Neither Valerie nor Nancy actually wanted to stay in Darwin, but Maisie was set on the idea.

She wanted me to book a hotel for them, at the art centre's expense, and change their flights back to Maningrida. I pointed out that there was no money to pay for a hotel, that they didn't have a way of getting around and that they would need money for taxis, buses and food. I wrestled with the problem all that day: they were adults who could do whatever they wanted and surely I shouldn't try and stop them. But at the same time, I felt the responsibility of a tour leader, and was anxious to get them home safely.

For a while Darwin was forgotten as we visited the Opera House and the Harbour Bridge, admiring the view and taking photos of the women in front of these icons. We went back to the hotel in the late afternoon, all of us exhausted. Valerie and I went out to get takeaway for dinner; once again I sought out fresh vegetables for myself, while she bought chicken and chips for herself and the others.

Later that night, Maisie decided to ring a friend in Darwin, hoping they could stay with him. He wasn't in so she left him a message; for me, it was the perfect outcome, delaying any decision until she could speak to him.

❧ ❧

Our last day in the big city was devoted to shopping. The women asked to be taken to 'secon' 'an' shops, so we went to Newtown, where I knew there were a couple of op shops. I was browsing through the racks, thinking I could do with some vintage winter clothes for the upcoming week in Melbourne, when I looked up to find that the others were hauling clothes off racks and shelves in bulk. They had brought some of their own spending money with them and didn't need to try anything on because they were buying for their families. I stood by, open-mouthed, as the shop assistant added up their purchases—an incredible total of $250 in a shop full of $1 and $2 price tags.

As we were getting ready to leave, organising everything in bags, the manager came up with a shopping trolley full of babies' and children's clothes, and told the women they could have it. She explained to me that she was donating it to them because she thought that the state of Aboriginal communities was shocking, and she wanted to do what she could to help. It was a kind gesture, but I was struck by the fact that this woman was so confident in assuming that Valerie, Nancy and Maisie were underprivileged because their hair, clothes and skin identified them as Aboriginal people from the bush. There was always plenty of cash around in Maningrida, and not much to spend it on. Money was not the primary source of the community's problems.

That night we had our final big city experience: dinner with Humphrey, who had organised the print exhibition. We met him at the gallery, where there was a function in the foyer—finger food and drinks, and lots of hip Sydney people standing around. Maisie, Nancy and Valerie stayed on the periphery of the action, choosing seats in a corner and keeping to themselves. It might have been their lack of English, or it might have been shyness or it could have been that they were simply not interested in talking to Balandas. Or it might have been that they felt so alienated by Sydney that it was difficult to interact with strangers.

Humphrey found us and came over.

'I bought a fish trap when I was in Maningrida, but I've been carting it around Sydney showing it to people and it's coming apart. I was thinking maybe one of you could take a look at it? Would that be OK?'

A flurry of Kuninjku as Valerie and Maisie explained the request to Nancy, and then we left the crowded foyer for the office, where the three women sat on the floor, and Nancy went to work on the trap. Then Humphrey showed them the dilly bags he had bought, and the women explained what fibres they were made from and how they were made. Valerie got up and modelled the way the dilly bag was traditionally worn, suspended from the head by its string handle. For about twenty minutes, Maisie, Nancy and Valerie were at the centre of their own experience. Instead of relying on me for translation and mediation of what was going on, the interaction was oriented around them. It was the only experience in the four days that relied on Kuninjku knowledge rather than Balanda knowledge.

Early the next morning we went to the airport and they boarded their plane. The issue of Darwin had been resolved by their exhaustion. They were all ready to go home.

∽ ∾

I got back to Maningrida a week later after attending a language conference in Melbourne. As soon as I got to the art centre I saw some distinctive new work: miniature versions of the usual sculptures in families of three or four. I was pleased to hear that it was Valerie's work. I had been worried that she might have a difficult time returning to Maningrida, thinking that she might even have left again by the time I got back. She must be doing well if she was being so creative.

The community newspaper had come out—photocopied A4 pages stapled together—with two pages full of photos of Elroy, Norris, Janey and Chelsea. The two girls had stopped coming to the centre, Janey coming in to explain that they were going to work at the nursery instead. But I started to see them around town: they were always together, often sitting on the grass outside a house or on the side of a road, their eyes red and blank from ganja. Sometimes they would acknowledge me and say hello; at other times they simply stared off into space. When we spoke, I could see that confidence and vitality had ebbed out of them, and they never met my eyes. The sheepish look of the stoned adolescent had become familiar to me now, and I had come to loathe its inertia and passivity.

A couple of days later there was a printmaking workshop—some of the staff from a printmaking gallery in Darwin had come out to teach people at the women's centre how to do linocuts. I went in to visit, and found Valerie there—the star artist, her work dazzling on the wall among the more amateur attempts of women who might never have done artwork other than weaving before. Her arm was out of its plaster cast, and she looked relaxed and healthy. She laughed at me for being so impressed by her work, but she was proud of it at the same time, aware that she was more prolific and innovative than she had ever been before.

Back at work, I was busy setting up the language program. The linguists were starting to arrive, and the money was going to be spent in time. The women I'd met in Alice Springs probably still didn't have any funding for their school-based language programs but Bawinanga would again perform the right bureaucratic tricks, qualifying us for more funding next time around.

Alice had recently been to a conference for Aboriginal art centres, where Maningrida had been held up as a 'benchmark organisation'. Our art centre was favoured because it was a well-managed business. George and Samson and Janey and Chelsea didn't come into the equation.

On Monday morning, I saw Valerie from a distance. My eye was caught by the white flash of a bandage on the arm that had just come out of its cast. She had obviously been bashed again.

Later, when I saw Nancy and Maisie at the art centre, I asked them what had happened. Laughing, they told me that she and Amos had been drunk and had a fight on the weekend. I couldn't see the funny side of it: their laughing just infuriated and bewildered me. I went back over everything I'd heard about the importance of family in Aboriginal cultures, and about women being protected by their male relatives from violence like this, and I thought angrily that none of this was true. I was angry with Amos and the other men in the family for not protecting her, and I was angry with Maisie and Nancy for laughing about it, and I was angry with everyone in the Kuninjku nation, and I was angry with everyone Aboriginal, and every Balanda as well because we were hopeless and inept and made no difference to anything, and I was angry with Maningrida itself, the dusty ground, the stinking hot weather, the river full of crocodiles. It was all relentless: there was no escape from any of it.

I thought all day about Nancy and Maisie's laughter. Eventually, I came to the conclusion that in a place like this, where violence was part of everyday life, laughing was not such a bad strategy. To laugh at something is to exert your power over it. Laughing can be akin to mocking and deriding, and this relies on the laugher having the power. So maybe when they laughed they were grabbing the power that was taken away from them when they were subjected to this violence. This seemed like a plausible theory, but it was horrible: were things in such a state that this theory was right? What kind of life was this?

When I saw Valerie a few days later, I made light of the situation. After all, I figured, my angst-ridden frowning sympathetic face wouldn't do her any good.

'Get behind Bob next time,' I joked. Bob was the biggest, fattest man in her family, if not in the whole community. I wanted her to know that I cared, but it was hard to know how to show it. There was nothing that I could do, and I didn't even understand the situation. I didn't know what Valerie wanted, how she felt about her life, what she thought about her husband and how he treated her, or whether she had started this most recent fight that had left him with bruises and her with broken bones. She was my friend and all I could do was wave from the sidelines of her life. So I made it a smiling, cheerful, happy kind of a wave.

❧ ❧

Later that day, I needed to speak to Jimmy about half a dozen paintings that we were sending off for an exhibition. In between reading old docos and writing new ones, and talking to artists about their work and checking my interpretation of what they had said in a dictionary, I now knew a lot about the artists and their work. After a year in my job, I generally knew the story of a work and who had painted it by its design. So I knew that Jimmy's paintings were all about the same thing—encrypted,

abstract designs referring to a secret, sacred ceremony. They
differed in composition and in detail: some showed a particular
plant linked to this ceremony; some were linked to a place called
Mukkamukka, others to Kakodbebuldi.

I began asking him about the details of the paintings—'So
that painting is about that ceremony?'

'Yo.'

'And these circles here, is that that bangkarl plant?'

'Yo.'

'At Mukkamukka?'

'Kakodbebuldi.'

'Yo, Kakodbebuldi.'

When we had finished I ended the conversation as I had
learnt to in Kuninjku: 'Ma. Kamak. Bony.' ('OK. Good. That's
enough.')

Jimmy nodded and agreed, 'Ma, bony.'

Then he walked towards the door, but just before opening
it and walking out he turned to me and smiled—the first smile
he had ever bestowed on me—and said, 'You speakim little bit
that Kuninjku,' and laughed and nodded. I smiled back and said,
'Yo, little bit.'

Ten

Dry Season was Balanda season. The non-Aboriginal population of the town expanded as contractors, researchers and visitors arrived. It was also the time of year for Bawinanga to set up its new enterprises. These business opportunities would bring money into the community, and were supposed to reduce the community's dependence on government funding in the long term. Bawinanga's hub of Balanda staff, who acted on behalf of the members to provide them with services, had extended operations to the provision of opportunities.

There were two kinds of enterprises. In some, Aboriginal land or sea was used by Balandas for commercial activity, and they returned a royalty to the owners of that territory. Under this scheme, there was a man running a barramundi fishing business, where tourists were flown into the town and taken out for a couple of days on his boat. He snap-froze the barramundi they caught so that they could take it home, a trophy of an authentic experience. It was generally agreed among the Balandas that this was a good scheme: it brought income in; it was managed tourism, which was surely where the economic future of Aboriginal people lay; and it was supported by the community.

I wasn't so sure. How different was this income to welfare? I wondered whether the community considered the difference between barra fishing royalties and the dole or cedeepee. Personally, I wasn't sure that there was any real difference. All the community had to do to get the royalty money was say yes.

The second kind of enterprise was intended to involve Aboriginal people more directly by setting up businesses that people in the community would work in. The latest example was a cosmetics company that wanted to use the fruit of a local tree for one of its products. They devised a plan where the trees would be planted on outstations, and Aboriginal people would harvest the fruit and sell it to the company at the market rate.

The most visible outcome of this project was the employment of Dan, Tommy's Balanda friend, who spent his days driving around to outstations planting trees. I was concerned that if Dan was doing all the planting, he might end up doing all the harvesting as well, and this would effectively become more sit down money. Usually, Balandas took up the slack when Aboriginal people drifted away from the work they had agreed to do. Dan defended the project when I asked him about it, saying that he thought it would work because people could earn money on their own country. Then, as he talked about what he was doing and which outstations were involved, Dan said that he was working with the Aboriginal people to 'try and make them own the work a bit'. This phrase came out of a community development model, where communities are given help to do things for themselves, rather than having things done for them. Back in Melbourne, I had been familiar with terminology like this, through friends who worked as social workers or were studying community development. Dan's words surprised me because I realised that I hadn't heard anything like this since arriving in Maningrida. Aside from Dan, none of the Balandas were qualified to help communities in this way; we came to Maningrida with an ad hoc array of skills, and we slotted into the Balanda machine, and kept on with the task of delivering services. In the fragment of Dan's sentence I caught a glimpse of what the alternatives might be.

෴ ෴

Although I had heard of terms like 'capacity building' and 'community development', I didn't know much about what they meant. I did know that organisations like Community Aid Abroad use a community development model in their aid to developing countries, and that it was based on teaching people to do something for themselves, rather than providing the service for them.

Like all the other Balandas in Maningrida, I provided a service for the community, but was not able to transfer my skills so that an Aboriginal person could take the job on. My good intentions, and conviction that it was important for the community to be more empowered and less reliant on Balandas, weren't enough.

I hadn't understood any of this when I arrived. I had expected to work alongside Aboriginal people, or to work at their direction. It didn't turn out to be like that, and my disillusionment had been painful. I thought about the ethos of some of the other Balandas, that we were doing a good thing for Aboriginal people by working on their behalf. This was a common view in Maningrida.

But I couldn't see that taking responsibility away from Aboriginal people—however benevolently it was done—was a good thing, because it meant taking power away as well. This opinion had built up slowly, over the months of living there, until it had become the basis of most of my interpretation of Maningrida.

Paradoxically, I now felt at home here. I was better at my job than I had been in the first six months; I was better at every aspect of living in Maningrida. I now had a small social life, I was much more comfortable with spending time alone and I was confident in my interactions with Aboriginal people and in the decisions I made at work.

But on the other hand, the role of Balandas in Maningrida seemed flawed to me, and I no longer wanted to be a part of it. We were not actively or directly damaging the community, and nearly all of the Balandas I knew were well intentioned, principled in the way they worked, and committed to doing the best they could for the community. But we were part of something that wasn't working, and that sometimes seemed indirectly to be making the problems worse. I was often depressed by the inertia in the community, and upset and angry about the levels of domestic violence and drug abuse—the most visible symptoms of social decay. I was frustrated by our inability to do anything that would actually make things better for Aboriginal people. It was emotionally draining to go to work every day in an 'Aboriginal community organisation' and work on behalf of the community, while all around the social problems got worse, literacy rates stayed low, gambling and drug addiction flourished in the town camps, and the next outbreak of violence or suicides was only a wet weekend away.

I'd learnt to live with the depressing, frustrating, upsetting realities of community life, as well as appreciating its fulfilling, encouraging and even everyday aspects. And now I wanted to move away from it, to a place where I would no longer need to cope with being so disheartened.

I knew that as soon as I left, someone else would step into my job. My presence had not changed anything and neither would my departure. I began to make plans to return to Melbourne in September, at the end of the Dry.

∽ ∾

A new book was recommended to me by a friend in Darwin: *Why Warriors Lie Down and Die*, by Richard Trudgen. It had an encouraging subtitle: 'Towards an understanding of why the Aboriginal people of Arnhem Land face the greatest crisis in health and education since European contact'. The book argued that the key to the appalling health and social conditions of the Yolngu people in east Arnhem Land was the failure of communication between them and white Australians. One of his examples particularly struck me.

White health workers were trying to educate Yolngu people about the five food groups, to promote healthy eating. After several years of failed attempts, the author learnt of the Yolngu food classification system. It put foods in two groups—basically meat and vegetables. It was common knowledge among Yolngu people that to be healthy, a person needed to eat both types of food. Once Richard Trudgen had learnt about this system, he could recast the education about five food groups based on the Yolngu system.

It was a good example of the pitfalls of cross-cultural education and how they can be overcome. The solution offered was training in Yolngu language and culture, and cross-cultural communication, for all non-Yolngu people working in Yolngu communities. But something about the book disconcerted me: the author's assumption that only white people can grapple with cultural clash. Perhaps he believed, deep down, that Aboriginal people could think only in Aboriginal terms. I had come to think that many Balandas think this way. Balandas don't believe this about themselves, however. According to their mind set, they possess the intelligence and ability to think creatively and to overcome cultural boundaries, whereas Aboriginal people need to have these things done for them.

But Aboriginal people in the Top End are experts at interacting with other cultures, such as the Makassan trepang fishers who had arrived on their shores every year for centuries. Arnhem Land is one of the most linguistically diverse regions in the world, and the different tribes and groups had lived alongside each other and maintained their distinct languages and cultures. Some analysts argued that their relationships had been violent, punctuated by raids where men were killed and women were captured; however, they had also developed elaborate diplomacy ceremonies to keep the peace and negotiate between the many different groups living relatively close together. From this perspective, they would seem better qualified than most white Australians in bridging a cultural gap.

The Balanda community in Maningrida was small. We tended to mix with our Balanda colleagues and to socialise at each other's houses because there were no public places where we could meet. Away from work, our social lives consisted of barbecues and dinner parties, with occasional trips out bush or out on someone's boat. Like most Balandas, I worked and lived within a group of about a dozen people. We saw each other at work all week, at dinner parties on Saturday nights, and again on the boat on Sundays. We all avoided conflict—we couldn't afford any rifts within such a small group.

So of course I'd been careful to avoid disagreement, tentatively offering my views to my fellow Balandas, and then backing quickly away when Alice, Mal or Archie disagreed. They were more experienced than I was. And they were my friends, and I respected them and their opinions. I had assumed that when we disagreed, they were right and I was wrong. Often, this meant that I didn't say much at all; I didn't want to disturb our fragile community. I was more open with Sue and Ron, who shared some of my opinions, but with other people I often listened to the conversations about Maningrida without voicing my concerns.

Once I had decided to leave, this changed. Archie came into my office and saw half a dozen bark paintings leaning against the walls. They were by an artist called Wally, but the designs were more abstract than his previous work, so Archie didn't recognise them. When I told him who had painted them, he responded with a story about Wally.

Bawinanga was building a house for Wally on his country. A site was chosen, and work was about to begin. Then a fight erupted within the Kuninjku community, and a different clan claimed the land where the house was to be sited. The two groups fought bitterly, neither willing to compromise, until the rival clan shot at a truck they thought Wally was driving. Wally and

Bawinanga chose a new, uncontroversial site for the house, and Wally and his family had lived there ever since.

Wally had always been charming in his interactions with me, even when politely refusing to come in and be interviewed. He struck me as highly intelligent. He spoke slowly, considering his words carefully, contemplating different descriptions and then settling on the most appropriate English words to explain his work and the meanings within it. He seemed strong-willed, possibly even stubborn, but gentle and thoughtful as well.

But Archie told me a different story. 'Bloody Wally's been humbugging me for years now to build him another house. He reckons he's sorted it all out with that other mob, so now he wants a new house on his own land. He thinks he can just leave the old one behind, and move into a new one.'

He went on to say that he had explained to Wally that because Bawinanga had already built him one house, he couldn't have another; but Wally refused to understand. 'He's in here nearly every week, humbugging me about it,' Archie said.

I wasn't sure what to make of this story: the Wally Archie knew was very different to the gentle, cerebral artist I had met.

As Archie got up to leave he said, 'It's the type of thing you've got to keep away from the people in Canberra. They just wouldn't understand it—an Aborigine with a perfectly good house asking for another one!'

I knew that Archie expected me to agree with him, to share the exasperation of us Balandas who stood between Canberra and Arnhem Land. Previously, I might have agreed, or said something non-committal. But today I said, 'Why can't you tell Canberra?'

'They'd have a fit! An Aborigine wanting a second house, when he's already got a perfectly good one! They just wouldn't understand.'

'But isn't it kind of important for the funding bodies to know how complicated things are in the communities?'

Archie shook his head. 'If we didn't keep that sort of thing to ourselves, there'd be no more houses for this mob.'

'Well . . . I don't know . . . maybe we need to let Aboriginal people know that these things have important consequences.'

'Ah, that's not how it works, Mary Ellen. You'll understand when you've been here a bit longer.'

I thought carefully about my reply, eventually settling on, 'Maybe.'

'When you're a bit older and you've been around as long as me, you'll realise that these people have to be protected from themselves.'

Nothing had changed. Even when I overcame my timidity to articulate my feelings and views, people like Archie, older and more experienced than I was, seemed to simply ignore what I had to say. I was a young woman who had been there less than a year, and my opinion didn't count.

❧ ❧

What Archie said confirmed my opinion. I now thought of our role in Maningrida as a kind of 'protection racket'—an unspoken conspiracy to let the outside world know only what we thought it should hear.

I knew that in other communities it worked differently. In some places, Aboriginal staff run community groups that fund projects with royalties or other income. Noel Pearson, an Aboriginal leader from Cape York, was well known for working to change the way his community was run—and for advocating an end to passive welfare dependency in Aboriginal communities, and the right of Aboriginal people to take responsibility for their own lives. He was the only commentator on Aboriginal affairs I read, while in Maningrida, whose views made sense to me.

At a dinner party one Saturday night, we began to talk about the latest enterprise, a new safari camp that Bawinanga was setting up. The plan was that tourists would come from all over the world to hunt buffalo. These 'trophy hunters' paid thousands to travel the globe killing huge beasts, taking home the head. Ironic, I thought, in a world where children are still taught to hunt for their dinner. Bawinanga had entered into an agreement— a joint enterprise—with a small company in Darwin, who would run the safaris. Bawinanga built huts for the hunters and filled them with rustic furniture and home comforts. This work was done by white people, and all the signatures on the contract were Balanda names. Despite this, the consensus around the table was that the safari camp was an excellent development.

'I don't know how I feel about it,' I confessed. 'Isn't it just another Balanda enterprise bringing money in for Aboriginal people?'

I was shouted down by Mal. 'The whole idea came from Owen!' he said. 'He came to Bawinanga with the idea, and he's been involved all along.'

Owen was a tall, lean young man, who was impressive because he seemed particularly fit, active, capable and smart. He had a white mother and had grown up out of the community. When he returned as an adult he tried twice as hard as his cousins to fit in. He seemed to have no time for the town-based culture, preferring to spend his time on an outstation. He had been away at ceremony for the last couple of months, so I knew that he couldn't have been closely involved in all of the preparations for the camp, but it seemed too confrontational to bring this up.

I tried to explain my doubts. 'The camp is going to employ Balanda staff, so the benefit to the community will be more sit down money. Shouldn't we be trying to get away from all that?'

'No, that's not right,' Mal replied. 'It's basically going to be run by Owen, and I think one Balanda, that guy who's been out there helping to set the place up.'

He sounded annoyed. I felt like a fly being gently swatted away. But I kept going.

'I thought there was going to be a cook, and a housemaid to look after the accommodation, and they would both be Balandas—isn't that what Archie was saying?'

This time Mal's voice was louder, and his reply was sharp: 'You're so cynical, Mary Ellen. Maybe it's time you had a holiday.'

I was exasperated. 'I'm not being cynical! It just seems likely that those kinds of jobs would go to Balandas. Every time there's a new idea or enterprise, there's a few new Balandas coming along with it.'

Alice said, 'That's enough out of you. Just be quiet!' She turned to Ron and asked about his fishing the day before.

I sat in an astonished silence. Their response was an indication of how badly I had transgressed the Balanda code of not being critical about what we were doing in the community. I was quiet for the rest of the evening, but I simmered with grief for the good intentions I had brought to Maningrida and then unequivocally lost. I spent the rest of the evening listening to the conversation from the outside. It was hard enough living every day surrounded by a community with problems that didn't have apparent solutions. It was even worse to be told not to talk about it.

A few weeks later, Owen returned from ceremony, and took an active role in the new enterprise. The first hunter arrived, and got his money's worth: he was saved from death by Owen, who shot a wild pig between the eyes as it mauled him. So the first customer took home a trophy and a story, and the safari camp was deemed a huge success. Everyone was predicting a great future for it.

Mal's opinion seemed to be vindicated. But alongside Owen, at the safari camp worked four Balandas. I wondered whether my friends remembered our conversation. Whether they did or not, we avoided such topics now. When I had tried to talk about my doubts, they had felt personally attacked, and I didn't want to create that tension again. I had gone back to keeping my ideas to myself.

Eleven

THE WEATHER BECAME HEAVIER AND MORE STIFLING AS MY departure drew near. I was deliberately leaving in the middle of September, before the Build Up began, but it seemed to have come early this year. As I walked back to work after lunch about a week before my departure, the air was thick with humidity and mosquitoes. I was in a hurry, trying to avoid being bitten, when I saw Samson near the bank. Realising I would be unlikely to see him again before I left, I went over to say goodbye.

'Bobo gapala,' he said. 'Have a good time in Melbourne.' I was pleased to see that he looked better than when I'd seen him last—healthier and more alert.

'Bobo Samson,' I replied. 'Take care of yourself.' It was a stilted, awkward farewell, almost redundant as we hadn't seen each other since he had left the art centre months before. I was disappointed that there wasn't much left of the connection we'd made while working together. I didn't know whether I would see him again, but I was grateful for the few months of working together that we'd had—he was smart and funny, I had enjoyed his company, and working with the cedeepee staff had made me feel less isolated at work.

I was excited about going home, but there were people and aspects of my life in Maningrida that I was sorry to be leaving behind. In among the complications and difficulties, there had been the pleasure of living alongside another culture. I'd spent a year observing the Aboriginal people in Maningrida, learning about their art, picking up a few words of their languages and glimpsing a few aspects of their cultures.

And, very slowly, I'd come to know a few of them. I thought about Samson, Valerie, Nellie, Elroy, Norris, Thelma, and the many artists I'd had conversations with. I thought about leaving these people and their cultures behind, and I knew that I was unlikely to be amongst them again, and unlikely to encounter many traces of them in my Melbourne life.

As I cleaned out my flat and packed my Maningrida life away, I came across a magazine I'd been sent a few months before. I flicked through the pages of glamorous celebrities, city scenes and reviews of films and restaurants, and a picture of a termite mound caught my eye—it was the orange-brown colour of the dirt in this part of Australia. It was an ad for a four-wheel drive, and the headline asked 'What is there left to discover?'

Below the termite mound, on an ochre background, was a 'tall tale and true' from the Bush Tucker Man. It was a story about camping on the road to Maningrida. He'd heard a wild buffalo near the creek and then 'all hell broke loose'—the buffalo was being mauled by a crocodile. 'Within ten minutes I was packed up, fire out, and off in the four-wheel drive. There was no way I was waiting for that hungry croc.' I knew the road he was talking about, and the two or three rivers that punctuated the expanse of dry scrub. I was bemused to see that on the pages of this magazine, Maningrida became the land of adventure, and the Bush Tucker Man was telling an archetypal frontier story about it.

I'd heard similar stories many times, from people who lived in Maningrida, or had visited, or lived there once, and had turned their experiences into tall tales like this. These accounts always puzzled me, because they didn't fit my experience of Maningrida. It wasn't an ochre-coloured frontier adventure for me or my friends and colleagues. It was everyday life.

I was leaving Maningrida in a week, and I knew that my stories would be untidy and even contradictory. I wasn't casting myself into the mythology of the frontier. I was confused. I couldn't find good endings for my stories; instead they unravelled in my hands. Maningrida defied the archetypal structure that demanded a beginning, a middle, and an end.

I'd spent a lot of time trying to overcome my doubts and uncertainties about this place, convinced that some more analysis would lead me to a definite truth, a right answer, or at least a coherent perspective. But I had come to accept that this quest would only limit my understanding. The most powerful learning and thinking I was capable of came from my doubts themselves. There were many answers to every question I was interested in, and finally I had learnt to give up sorting through the answers to find or create a single, unified, consistent story.

It was difficult for a Balanda to live in Maningrida, though slightly easier if you could construct a coherent story about the community and your place in it. I had noticed that the people who had been there a long time preferred to speak in absolutes. They dealt in answers rather than questions, and they had created firm ground to stand on.

Reading the words of the Bush Tucker Man, I understood that my failure to create a story for myself might have been part of why I had to leave.

∽ ∾

With only a few days left in Maningrida, I set out to find Valerie so that I could say goodbye to her. I had asked Alice to let me know if she came into the art centre, but she hadn't seen her. Eventually I learnt that she was out of town at a big ceremony that was going to last at least another week, and was unlikely to come into town before I left. I was fond of Valerie, and worried about her future—whether she stayed in Maningrida with her husband, or went to Darwin to drink again. It was frustrating that I hadn't known about the ceremony in time to say goodbye to her properly, and I realised I would have to be content with leaving a message for her with Alice.

On my last day at work, we gathered round for afternoon tea, a Maningrida version of the standard Balanda office departure ritual. I stood in the art centre with the current staff: Elroy, Norris and Alice. We drank tea and ate cake and made small talk, and I kept thinking how strange it was that tomorrow I would catch a plane to Darwin for the last time.

I was given two presents: a beautifully woven pandanus mat that I had admired when it had come in, and an oddly shaped, knobbly parcel. I opened it to find two small carved dolphins, their bodies painted with the cross-hatched pattern typical of the region. I laughed at them, realising that Alice had given them to me because I often joked that the culture office was researching 'Aboriginal peoples' spiritual connection with dolphins'. These jokes referred to a request the art centre had received from someone wanting to study this topic. To me, it epitomised one aspect of positive racism, the tendency of some Balandas to ascribe to Aboriginal people their own hippy, new age ideas about crystals or dolphins or environmentalism.

The carvings had been made by an artist who'd recently arrived in the community, and they were the only depiction of dolphins I saw in my time there. Alice gave them to me as a joke; but in a way, they were the perfect memento of what I had learned.

I said goodbye to Elroy and Norris. I didn't have close emotional ties to these men, but I had enjoyed my slowly evolving relationships with them and was sad to be leaving them. 'Don't you worry,' Norris said. 'You still be here, walkin' all around this place. Your spirit, you know. You be here, walkin' everywhere, all around' he continued, gesturing around the art centre with his arm. 'We won't forget.'

∽ ∾

The next day was my last in Maningrida. I was booked on the 5 p.m. plane, and I was having lunch with my friends at 12.30. I spent the morning doing the final bits of cleaning and packing. I was alone in my flat, as I had been for so many hours of the past year. I had lain on the couch and struggled to make sense of this community; I had made desserts to take to Saturday night dinner parties; I had wished to be somewhere else; I had enjoyed being here. I looked around, every detail familiar to me, and knew that when I thought of Maningrida in the future I would think of this flat, these two rooms, and the thinking and learning that had taken place here.

At lunch, we spent hours eating and drinking on the verandah of Ron and Sue's house with the rivermouth gleaming behind us and kids playing on its banks. I knew that I was going, and I was looking forward to returning to my Melbourne life. But I was still there, in Maningrida, still immersed in the people and the work, still thinking of my flat as home, still able to navigate its corners in the dark, waking up in the morning and being certain of where I was. The real departure would happen slowly, over the following months; gradually, the details of Maningrida would slip away, to be replaced by details from my new life. For my first few nights in Melbourne, I would wake disoriented, my body's memory of furniture and steps and corners confounded by a new geometry it was yet to master.

I drove to the airport with my friends. I was the only passenger on the Sunday afternoon service, and the plane was a tiny twelve-seater with several of the seats removed to make way for freight. As it lifted off the tarmac, I looked out the window and watched the town recede. My friends stood in a small clump leaning over the cyclone mesh fence, waving. The town was dusty and brown, growing ever smaller as the little plane rose. The rivermouth looked blue and spectacular and inviting, but of course hosted at least one crocodile. I had become so used to this plane trip that I had often read a book rather than looking out the window. Today I was aware that it might be the last time I took this flight, and I was prepared to pay attention. But the view was soon obscured by cloudscape.

Epilogue

SOMETIMES I FELT THAT THE BEST I COULD SAY OF THE ROLE OF Balandas in Maningrida was that we were paternalistic. The worst was that the system we worked within prevented Aboriginal people from taking responsibility for themselves and their communities. They could choose not to send their children to school, and we would nod sagely and agree that Balanda schooling was not culturally relevant.

Before I went to Maningrida, I would have argued that indigenous systems of power and prestige were more important for indigenous people. If they ignored dominant culture schooling to spend time in ceremonial education, becoming fully fledged knowledgeable members of their own cultures, then that was a valid alternative.

But it didn't work like that, and the Balanda endeavour to protect the Aboriginal communities wasn't working. All sorts of aspects of the dominant culture were creeping into theirs—

drugs, unhealthy foods, television. Some children missed school for ceremony or hunting. But many spent their days sitting, stoned and hyped up on sugar, in front of television shows and Hong Kong action videos. We needed to think carefully about what it was that we were protecting.

We handed over the things we believed to be benign— housing, health care, cars, clothes—but with them came drugs, processed food, televisions and guns. We believed that Aboriginal cultures would be corrupted by contact with the intellectual aspects of Balanda culture—the English language, literacy and bureaucracy. We had fallen prey to the idea that a thing was just a thing, that it did not come with any culture attached. So we thought that a t-shirt that said 'Just do it' carried nothing more than its strands of cotton. But a teacher who said 'Keep trying' carried the weight of the colonial endeavour, assimilation and denigration. We were throwing the muck of our culture over the border between black and white, and keeping for ourselves the good stuff, all that is good and rich and strong. We kept sharing the beads and the mirrors, but the written version of the contract remained secret whitefella business.

The Balanda ethos of protection guided a lot of the work we did. But there was an unstoppable flow of the dominant culture into the Aboriginal world. At the same time, the traditional Aboriginal cultures were changing, not always for the better. The protection racket was not doing the communities any good.

What were the alternatives? I didn't have any answers. But I wondered whether, if we abandoned the idea that Aboriginal people should simply 'be Aboriginal', we might be able to work together to come up with a more realistic way of negotiating the constant, complex and inevitable processes of cultural exchange and interaction.

I remembered something that happened on the trip to Sydney, on our second night, at the opening of the exhibition. As I walked among the crowd with Valerie, she helped me practice Kuninjku with a simple conversation that went something like this:

'Sister!'

'Sister!'

'We're going inside?'

'Yes, we're going inside.'

'Good?'

'Good.'

'OK.'

'OK.'

After a while, as we walked with everyone else towards the stage for the speeches, she whispered in English, 'Those Balandas hear you speaking Kuninjku and . . .' She finished the sentence with an exaggerated look of amazement on her face, mimicking the way Balandas reacted to her, and then she laughed her head off.

I remembered looking at her in astonishment. She was playing with the notion of Aboriginal mystique. She knew what the Balandas thought about her, and about themselves: she was onto us.

Acknowledgements

THANKS TO JOHN HIRST, WHO SUGGESTED I WRITE ABOUT Maningrida and then gave me a job so that I could afford to do so; he also saw a book in what I was writing long before I did, and introduced it to its publisher. I am very grateful for all of his assistance, support and encouragement.

I am also grateful to Andrew Weldon, for unwavering faith in the book and in me; and to Kristie Dunn and Lorien Kaye for their friendship and for helping in hundreds of ways with this project. Andrew, Kristie, and Lorien all read drafts and gave me invaluable feedback and encouragement. Thanks also to all of my friends and family for many conversations about Maningrida and about the book.

At Allen & Unwin, I am particularly grateful to Claire Murdoch, who read the first draft responded enthusiastically, and to Karen Gee, who looked after the book in the crucial editing and production phases with great skill and sympathy;

and also to Elizabeth Weiss and Colette Vella. Thanks also to Sue Grose-Hodge for her editing which improved the book considerably.

Finally, my thanks to my friends and family who helped me in innumerable ways with the Maningrida experience, both those in the town and those who telephoned, emailed, visited and sent letters and parcels from outside.

Some of the ideas and stories in this book have appeared in different versions in the following previously published pieces: 'Separate and Unequal' in 'News Extra', *The Age*, Saturday 21 April 2001; 'Letter from Maningrida', *Australian Book Review*, June 2001; and 'Maningrida', *Best Australian Essays 2001*, edited by Peter Craven (Melbourne: Black Inc).